Reflections of
1776
The Colonies Revisited

Reflections of 1776

1776

The Colonies Revisited

NANCY SIRKIS

Text by Ellwood Parry

A Studio Book · THE VIKING PRESS · New York

For

Andrew and Daniel

Other books by Nancy Sirkis

Newport: Pleasures and Palaces

Boston

One Family

Photographs and Captions Copyright © 1974 by Nancy Sirkis
Text Copyright © 1974 by The Viking Press, Inc.
All rights reserved
First published in 1974 by The Viking Press, Inc.
625 Madison Avenue, New York, N.Y. 10022
Published simultaneously in Canada by
The Macmillan Company of Canada Limited
SBN 670–59256–0
Library of Congress catalog card number: 73–20666
Printed in U.S.A.

Acknowledgments

It would have been impossible to complete this project without a tremendous amount of help and advice from many sources. First I would like to thank Abbott Lowell Cummings who was most generous with his time and advice. I am also grateful to Eliot Fremont-Smith, in whose company the idea for the book originated; and to Gerald Watland for his advice and help in locating Dutch Colonial buildings.

I am indebted to the following societies, foundations, and museums: the American Swedish Historical Foundation and Museum, Philadelphia, Pennsylvania; the Anne Arundel County Historical Society, Baltimore, Maryland; the Society of Colonial Dames of Philadelphia, Pennsylvania; Colonial Williamsburg, Inc., Williamsburg, Virginia; the Concord Antiquarian Society, Concord, Massachusetts; Germantown Historical Society, Germantown, Pennsylvania; Historic Deerfield, Deerfield, Massachusetts; the Huguenot Historical Society, New Paltz, New York; the Ipswich Historical Society, Ipswich, and the Marblehead Historical Society, Marblehead, Massachusetts; the Milford Historical Society, Milford, Connecticut; the Monmouth County Historical Association, Monmouth, New Jersey; the Mount Vernon Ladies' Association of the Union, Mount Vernon, Virginia.

Also, the Newport Historical Society and the Newport Restoration Foundation of Newport, Rhode Island; Old Gaol Museum of York, Maine; Old Salem, Inc., Winston-Salem, North Carolina; the Pennsylvania Historical and Museum Commission and the Philadelphia Museum of Art, Philadelphia, Pennsylvania; the Passaic County Park Commission, Paterson, New Jersey; Portsmouth Historical Society, Portsmouth, New Hampshire; Sleepy Hollow Restorations, Tarrytown, New York; the United States Department of the Interior; Wethersfield Historical Society, Wethersfield, Connecticut; the Whitefield House Museum, Nazareth, Pennsylvania; and the Henry Francis du Pont Winterthur Museum, Winterthur, Delaware.

Space does not permit me to list the many people who generously allowed me to photograph their homes, but I would like to take this opportunity to thank them all.

Last, I would like to thank my husband, Frank Horch, without whose help, encouragement and enthusiasm this book would never have become a reality.

N. S.

Contents

TITLE PAGE: Capitol, Colonial Williamsburg, Virginia.
OPPOSITE: Kitchen floor of the Hammond–Harwood House, Annapolis, Maryland.

Introduction

The intent of this book is to offer a glimpse of how the thirteen original colonies appeared when they became the United States of America almost two hundred years ago. It attempts to capture something of the look and feel of the colonies, from the time of their settlement until they became an independent nation in 1776. It is not intended to be a comprehensive technical study of colonial architecture and artifacts.

While traveling up and down the eastern seaboard, I tried to photograph the remnants of colonial America as they would have looked in 1776, eliminating as many of the encroachments of the twentieth century as possible and emphasizing the weather as part of the total atmosphere surrounding these buildings. Thus some beautiful and important buildings were eliminated because it was not always possible to escape telephone poles, paved sidewalks, and ugly signs stating the price of admission. Wherever signs of the twentieth century dominate the seventeenth- or eighteenth-century scene, the building was excluded; for examples, both Faneuil Hall and the Old State House in Boston are not included because there is no way to prevent their being dwarfed in photographs by surrounding skyscrapers. This is not to imply that this book is completely free of anachronisms—there are some, but I trust they are unobtrusive enough not to destroy the mood of any picture.

I wanted very much to emphasize the changing of the seasons, especially winter. Harsh New England winters were very much a part of the early settler's life, but these same harsh winters force the closing of many of the remaining historic houses today long before the snow falls, and so I could not include as many winter scenes as I would have liked.

The process of selecting the material to be photographed had other pitfalls as well. I began this book as a purist determined to photograph only original buildings. But how much of a house could be restored before it became a reconstruction? It soon became clear that the dividing line between restoration and reconstruction was usually vague, even indefinable; although I tried to emphasize houses that were minimally restored, here and there a few reconstructions have crept in. With a few notable exceptions, such as Mount Vernon, everything in this book predates 1776. But houses are not static entities; they change from owner to owner and grow with additions over the generations, and so a cutoff date of 1776 was sometimes impossible to observe faithfully in the strictest sense.

On the positive side, the buildings and artifacts appearing in this book were chosen for a rich variety of reasons: their architectural importance, their placement in an unspoiled, relatively unchanged setting, and their social significance in reflecting the art, culture, and atmosphere of the period. Most of the artifacts were photographed in colonial houses, in their natural environment, rather than on shelves in museums. The photographer looking for strong visual images and an architectural historian looking for the best and most significant examples may disagree over many selections, but compromises can be made so that a book like this one will be more thorough than just a collection of pretty pictures and more interesting to look at than a very technical catalogue. I have emphasized strong images here, but the reader will also find some photographs that serve only to provide information vital for the basic understanding of elementary aspects of colonial architecture.

Although this book started out being primarily concerned with architecture, I soon found that houses and details of houses did not always capture as much of the flavor of the times as I wished, so I began to photograph still lifes, toys, small personal items, furniture, utensils, and other fascinating objects to fill the gap.

As colonial America was not electrified, I used natural light wherever possible. And since Ellwood Parry and I both felt that the regional differences in colonial architecture were both interesting and significant, the book is divided in that way.

Finally, I hope that I have not left the impression that this was a grim undertaking. Sitting in the library doing research, waiting in the darkness of early morning in Georgia for dawn to break in order to capture the essence of a Southern plantation, coming across some small household object as sophisticated in concept as anything we have in the twentieth century, taking delight in looking at houses and objects made at a time when people took pride in their work—everything has been a fascinating experience. I hope the reader will feel and share in some of the excitement of discovery that I experienced in making this journey into America's past.

Nancy Sirkis
New York, 1974

Preface

It has been a pleasure to be included in this project, especially since my involvement came at the invitation of a friend whose photography I deeply admire. Too many books on colonial America are illustrated with photographs that look as if they had been taken by a real estate agent wielding a pocket Polaroid. The resulting images contain only the superficial, unimaginative, market-value facts about a particular historic building—and never the true spirit or feeling of actually living in that house at a particular moment in time.

What I have written as an accompaniment to Nancy Sirkis's photographs and captions is intended to be neither a rival in prose to the poetry of her pictures nor a prosaic textbookish history of colonial life. Instead, the very short three-part essay that follows in response to the photographs touches on some aspects of the material culture of the American colonies from the early seventeenth century until 1775–1776. The limited length and format do not permit the inclusion of full scholarly apparatus, but whenever possible I have mentioned the names of leading authorities in connection with their contributions to our understanding of early American arts and crafts, architectural design, and town planning. For those interested in further reading, a number of informative and useful books are listed in a brief bibliography at the end.

E. P.

I

NEW ENGLAND

At the opening of the seventeenth century one of several English mariners to explore the Atlantic coast of what was then called Northern Virginia was Captain John Smith. Unlike the others, however, he actively encouraged the plantation of a colony on the land he renamed New England. In the obviously commercial nature of his voyage of discovery in 1614 and throughout his subsequent book, *A Description of New England* (London, 1616), one finds heavy traces of the three basic motivations—easy profit, national pride, and religious zeal—that would inspire so many Europeans to settle in the New World.

Captain Smith arrived along the coast of New England in April 1614. He came as the master of two ships, outfitted by London merchants, and his first objective was to turn a quick profit for these financial backers. In the explorer's own words, "our plot was there to take Whales and make tryalls of a Myne of Gold and Copper," but, when both of these ventures proved impractical, "Fish and Furres," a far less lucrative cargo for the return voyage, were a necessary refuge in order to cover the original investment. So, while the main party of English sailors set to work catching and drying cod, herring, and mullet by the hundredweight during the spring and summer of 1614, Captain Smith and a few others who shared his adventurous spirit ranged the coast in a small boat, offering trifles to the more friendly savages in exchange for valuable beaver skins and otter pelts.

At the same time, Captain Smith was able to draw up an accurate chart of the New England coast—to go with his earlier map of Virginia (1612). This new chart of the northern territory claimed by the English crown was clearly based on extensive observations of the many harbors, wooded islands, rocky points, sandbanks, shoals, and other littoral landmarks from Penobscot Bay to Cape Cod, but no map or navigational chart alone could picture the beauty and potential fertility of the land or the riches of the sea extending out to the Grand Banks. That required spoken and written words.

At the opening of his book, describing New England, Captain Smith claimed that "of all the foure parts of the world that I have seene not inhabited, could I have but meanes to transport a Colonie, I would rather live here then any where." Even without extensive inland explorations in 1614, New England seemed to offer everything needed for the success of a new colony. Other

A corner in the Buckman Tavern, Lexington, Massachusetts.

explorers had labeled the region a "cold, barren, mountainous, rocky Desart," unfit for English habitation, but Captain Smith assured his readers that there were "all sorts of excellent good woodes for building houses, boats, barks or shippes; with an incredible abundance of most sorts of fish, much fowle, and sundry sorts of good fruites for man's use." Furthermore, there was plentiful game in the forests, a temperate climate, and numerous Indian "Gardens and Corne Fields" along the coast to testify to the quality of the soil.

As a major spokesman for English colonization efforts, Captain Smith had two objectives: to attract wealthy investors with the promise of substantial capital gains and to interest men of good spirits but limited means in the idea of future emigration. What could provide greater moral and spiritual contentment, he reasoned, than for a relatively poor man, able to advance his station in life only through his own merits, to make a living from the fresh ground purchased at the hazard of his own life in the wilderness of North America?

> If [a man] have but the taste of virtue, and magnanimitie, what to such a minde can bee more pleasant, than planting and building a foundation for his Posteritie, gotte from the rude earth, by Gods blessing and his own industrie, without prejudice to any? If hee have any graine of faith or zeale in Religion, whan can hee doe lesse hurtfull to any; or more agreeable to God, then to seeke to convert those poore Salvages to know Christ . . . ? What so truely sutes with honour and honestie, as the discovering things unknown? erecting Townes, peopling Countries, informing the ignorant, reforming things unjust, teaching virtue; and gaine to our Native mother-countrie a kingdom to attend her . . . ?

Aside from a few scattered outposts and fishing stations along the New England coast, the first major settlement between Cape Ann and Cape Cod was established by Englishmen who had the strongest reasons for emigration. Before settling at New Plymouth in December 1620, the Pilgrims had lived in Holland for twelve years to avoid religious persecution for their radical separatist ideas. There is some evidence to believe that while a few Pilgrim delegates were negotiating in London (1617–1620) for the necessary patent from the Virginia Company and for a seven-year financial agreement with a group of merchants, some thought was given to hiring John Smith as the ship's captain and experienced guide for the trip to the New World. This idea was soon abandoned, however, either because the explorer's fee was too high for their limited means or because, as a former governor of the Virginia Colony, Captain Smith was too closely connected with the Jamestown settlement. The Pilgrims, who were simple artisans, farmers, and laborers from East Anglia, did not trust the Anglican (Church of England) colony in Virginia, founded by "knights, Gentlemen, Merchants and other Adventurers of London and else where." They feared a corruption of the purity of their beliefs or else a return of persecution if they settled too near Jamestown, and yet they were also afraid of establishing themselves too far from any common defense or supply base.

After many costly delays in port, the *Mayflower* set out on September 6, 1620, for the long two-month voyage across the treacherous North Atlantic. Landfall was reached off Cape Cod in the second week of November, but when an attempt was made to go south to their real destination at the mouth of the Hudson River, head winds and terrifying shoals turned them back to the safety of Provincetown Harbor. And there, according to William Bradford, the Pilgrims "fell upon their knees and blessed the God of heaven, who had brought them over the vast and furious ocean, and delivered them from all the periles and miseries thereof, againe to set their feete on the firme and stable earth, their proper elemente."

Before any of the Pilgrim fathers actually went ashore to explore Cape Cod, a compact was drawn up by the leaders aboard the *Mayflower* and signed by all the adult males in the company. Since the patent from the Virginia Company was useless so far north, this new document took its place by providing for a responsible civil government that would enjoy the submission and obedience of all free men under its jurisdiction. Unmistakably, as Samuel Eliot Morison has pointed out, the Mayflower Compact, like the Virginia Assembly, was "an almost startling revelation of the capacity of Englishmen in that era for self-government" and of their determination, in fact, "to live in the colonies under the rule of law."

Beyond their innate respect for law and orderly process, however, the "100 and odd persons" who landed at New Plymouth were not well equipped for the task of starting a colony in the midst of winter. And they had "no friends to wellcome them, nor inns to entertaine or refresh their weather-beaten bodys, no houses or much less townes to repaire too, to seeke for succoure." On the twenty-fifth day of December they began to erect the first building for communal use, a storehouse to receive them and their goods, but the very job of unloading the *Mayflower*, at anchor in the harbor, and transferring their stores to the Common House was made more difficult by the want of small boats, the foulness of the weather, and the growing number of men too sick to work.

A few able-bodied colonists had "begune some small cottages for their habitation" as time and weather would permit, but this halting effort was far from enough to provide adequate shelter for all. Compared to the moderate climate of the British Isles, winter in New England proved "sharp and violent" in the extreme, a season "subject to cruell and feirce storms" that could descend without warning. "Wanting houses and other comforts" in the depth of winter and "being infected with the scurvie and other diseases" from their long voyage, it is not surprising that half the Pilgrims died in two or three months' time after landing, sometimes at the rate of two or three a day. By the end of February "scarce 50 remained," and out of that number only about six or seven were well enough to care for the others and nurse them back to health.

The return of spring in 1621 brought improving health and better spirits to the infant colony, and some construction work resumed, although the chief priority was planting corn. Luckily, the Pilgrims had chosen to settle on a hill above Plymouth Harbor that had once been the site of an Indian village. The land was already cleared, saving the colonists a great deal of time and trouble, but even more importantly, the site had also been abandoned, so no hostile band of Wampanoag warriors appeared to drive the English settlers back to their ship. Just in case of a surprise attack, though, a blockhouse was built at the top of the hill in the summer of 1622; it contained a large room, used for religious services (a precursor of the New England meetinghouse), and a platform above for the "ordinance" (meaning several cannon to control the approaches to the village in times of danger).

With a degree of military security assured by the blockhouse and by a palisade around the entire settlement, domestic comforts could be attended to. In the years that followed, the Pilgrims ("with the Lord's blessing") gradually transformed all the makeshift wigwam, hut, and hovel-like shelters of their first winters into "orderly, fair, and well-built houses," each with a fenced-in garden or orchard behind it. From the outset these small dwellings, flanking the main street at Plymouth, were not log cabins—that "myth" was dispelled long ago—but timber-frame, post-and-beam structures in the manner of rural houses and cottages in southeastern England.

At almost exactly the same moment in London, it should be remembered, Italian Renaissance ideas of architectural order and decoration were first introduced in the design of the Banqueting House, Whitehall (1619–1622), by Inigo Jones, and before the end of the 1620s Charles I had commissioned Rubens, the leading baroque painter in northern Europe, to create a series of nine huge allegorical scenes for the ceiling of this new building. By contrast to these courtly arts, the humble unadorned houses of the English colonists in the New World revealed their medieval ancestry. The basic crafts involved in building a simple wood-frame house had changed very little in four centuries. In effect, the first comparatively substantial dwellings at Plymouth Plantation were no more elaborate than the wooden chests in which the Pilgrims stored their belongings and valuables, but they were far more flammable since the traditional thatched roofs (before wood shingles became mandatory) caught on fire all too frequently.

Of equal importance, next to the question of immediate shelter and military defense, was the matter of an adequate food supply. In this regard it was extremely fortunate for the Pilgrims that a few Indians came forward to act as friendly guides and interpreters. The famous story of Squanto teaching the settlers how to fish and how to plant corn is now as legendary as the friendship of Massasoit, the Wampanoag sachem, and his participation in the first Thanksgiving feast along with many of his braves.

In terms of its economic position, the Plymouth community made little progress until it could feed and house itself properly. In the spring of 1621 the *Mayflower* had returned to England empty—much to the consternation of the colony's creditors in London—but no one, not even the ship's crew, had been well enough during the preceding winter to gather a cargo of any kind. When the *Fortune* unexpectedly arrived at Plymouth with thirty or so more settlers in November 1621, it stayed only a fortnight before sailing home, loaded "as full as she could stowe" with excellent split-oak clapboard and many beaver skins.

At first the forests of New England must have seemed unlimited, making timber a major commodity for export, but the local need for firewood and building materials was insatiable—almost to the point of exhausting readily available supplies. As early as 1626 the Plymouth Colony passed a law forbidding the export of planks, boards, and beams for frame houses in order to prevent the complete destruction of all the hardwood trees in the vicinity. Because of this restriction on timber, the Pilgrims had to concentrate on furs to pay off their indebtedness. By

1627 they had set up an outpost at Aptucxet to trade with the Wampanoags and with the Nauset Indians on Cape Cod. To the north their trading station (1628) on the Kennebec River (Maine) was meant to drain off some of the wealth in skins that usually went to the French in Canada, while their western outpost on the Connecticut River (1633) provided an alternative marketplace to compete with the Dutch settlements in the upper Hudson Valley. Finally, by the end of 1633, the Plymouth Colony was out of debt and could begin to make a sizable profit from the fur trade for itself as long as American supplies and European demand lasted.

The Pilgrim fathers may have been the first to settle on the New England coast, but their "plantation" was soon eclipsed in size and importance by the Massachusetts Bay Colony. Officially known as "The Governor and Company of the Massachusetts Bay in New England," this new political unit held a patent to all the land from three miles south of the Charles River to three miles north of the Merrimac and extending inland from the Atlantic coast to the vaguely defined "South Sea." When a royal charter was granted by Charles I in 1629, giving the new company undisputed title to this land as well as administrative autonomy, the stage was set for the "Great Migration" of thousands of English Puritans, eager to escape the enmity of Archbishop Laud and determined to establish their own Christian community ("a city upon a hill") for the world to see in the New Canaan or Promised Land of the New World.

One of the initial acts of the Massachusetts Bay Company, once its royal charter had been signed in 1629, was to commission an official seal from a London silversmith, a seal that could be stamped in hot wax on important colony documents to verify their authenticity. From the first, the design on this seal included the full name of the company in Latin and a stylized Indian, holding a bow in one hand and an arrow in the other, while speaking the words "Come Over and Help Us." Naturally, this invitation was taken from the King James version of the Bible and not from any spokesman for the aboriginal tribes of North America. According to Acts 16:9, the Apostle Paul was traveling in Asia Minor when a vision suddenly appeared to him in the night; a man of Macedonia stood before him, beseeching him to "Come over to Macdonia and help us." On the spot Paul decided to go on to Macedonia, convinced that God had called him to preach the gospel there.

If, by means of this seal, the missionary impulse was meant to be a highly visible aspect of the Puritans' "Errand into the Wilderness," serious civilizing and Christianizing efforts among the Indians enjoyed a very low priority in the Bay Colony's affairs during the first two decades of its existence. When Governor John Winthrop arrived at Naumkeag (Salem) in 1630, bringing the official seal with him, his major concern was for the welfare of all the Englishmen under the jurisdiction of the "General Court"—that included the earlier settlers at Salem and Charlestown as well as the thousand more emigrants who landed in the early part of 1630. Faced with the question of survival, no one had time for the godly task of saving souls among the fewer than five hundred Massachusetts Indians who lived in scattered villages within the patent. John Eliot, the "Apostle to the Indians," did not deliver his first sermon in Algonquian until 1646, and the principal "praying towns" for savages who embraced Christianity, towns such as Natick, Punkapog, and Nashobah, were not established until after 1650.

The wilderness Zion envisioned by Governor Winthrop and his followers in 1630 could never have been a single City of God due to the very mundane problems of food supply. As increasing numbers of Puritans, fleeing the political and religious unrest that led up to the English Civil War, poured into Massachusetts Bay, expansion of the colony took the form of proliferating villages at key points along the shore or along the inland waterways. There were no large farms or fishing fleets at first to support a growing urban population. Only the village system—with closely grouped houses surrounded by newly cleared fields—allowed for adequate defense in addition to easy access to the crops that had to be carefully tended by hand.

Thanks to William Wood's account, entitled *New England's Prospect* (London, 1634), we have an extremely early eyewitness narrative of what the Bay Colony looked like in 1629–1634. In the process of describing "that part of *America*, commonly called New England," Wood left an extensive word picture "of the severall plantations" in the area of the patent—chief among them were the following:

Wessagusett (Weymouth)—"the outmost plantation in the patent to the Southward," a pleasant and healthful village; its Indian name was soon changed to an English one.

Dorchester—"which is the greatest Towne in New England; well woodded and watered; very good arable grounds, and Hay-ground, faire Corne-fields, and pleasant Gardens, with Kitchin-gardens: In this plantation is a great many Cattle, as Kine, Goats, and Swine." There was also a reasonable harbor, and "the inhabitants of this towne . . . the first that set upon the trade of fishing in the Bay . . . received so much fruite of their labours, that they encouraged others to the same undertakings."

Roxbury—"a faire and handsome Countrey-towne; the inhabitants of it being all very rich."

Boston—two miles northeast from Roxbury, had an excellent situation, "being a Peninsula," but there were certain disadvantages to this site, according to Wood. "Their greatest wants be Wood, and Medow-ground, which never were in that place." On the other hand, "it being a necke and bare of wood, they are not troubled with three great annoyances of Woolves, Rattlesnakes, and Musketoes."

Charlestown—on the north side of the Charles River, "well paralel'd with her neighbour Boston."

Medford—on a great creek not far from Charlestown, "a very fertile and pleasant place, and fit for more inhabitants than are yet in it."

Newtown (Cambridge)—"one of the neatest and best compacted Townes in New England, having many faire structures, with many handsome contrived streets. . . . This place was first intended for a City, but upon more serious consideration it was not thought so fit, being too farre from the Sea."

Mystic—"seated by the waters side very pleasantly; there be not many houses as yet."

Saugus—six miles north-northeast of Boston Harbor; and lastly:

Salem—"which stands on the middle of a necke of land very pleasantly." Even though "where most of the houses stand is very bad and sandie ground, yet for seaven years together it hath brought forth exceeding good corne, by being fished [the Indian method of placing a fish in the earth to act as fertilizer under each hill of corn] but every third yeare; in some places is very good ground, and very good timber, and divers springs hard by the sea side. Here likewise is a store of fish, [such] as Basses, Eeles, Lobsters, Clammes, &c."

In keeping with modern interests in the evolution of town planning and urban design in America, several architectural historians have gone back to original maps and documents of the Puritan era to rediscover the common pattern on which virtually all New England communities were organized before the Revolutionary War. Local differences in terrain, we are told, might have an effect on minor details of the basic layout, but not on the fundamental aspects of the plan. Within the Bay Company patent, specific quantities of land could be obtained by groups of freemen (called proprietors) either by purchase or by direct grant from the General Court. In Massachusetts this entire parcel of land was called a town—a less misleading term would have been township—and somewhere within its clearly defined borders the new proprietors would select the best location for their village.

At the center of each new village community was a common or village green, on which (or next to which) the meetinghouse would be erected as the first public building. Around the central open space and along the streets leading into it, home sites were carefully marked out and then apportioned as fairly as possible among the purchasers or grantees according to such variable factors as the nature of each man's profession, the size of his family, or the amount of his initial investment. In the town of Topsfield, Massachusetts, for example, the young, recently married pastor of the local congregation, Joseph Capen, received one of the choicest sites available to build his parsonage. At the top of a slight rise, facing the village green and not far from the site of the original meeting house, the Parson Capen House survives (restored 1913) where it was erected in June 1683.

Once cleared of tree stumps and rocks, the fields around a new village were also divided into long strips and assigned to the various proprietors according to a similar formula. At the same time, some of the arable lands, like some of the building sites, were not immediately given to individual owners but were held in common—perhaps to be sold at a future time to a limited number of newcomers to the town. In practice, since the layout of each village was a closed system that could not accommodate large numbers, this type of plan actually encouraged the creation of still more towns, deeper and deeper into the wilderness. Furthermore, following familiar English precedents, each of these communities also retained title to common grazing lands (keeping the livestock out of the field crops and kitchen gardens) and common woodlands (where no tree could be felled for profit without prior consent from the village elders).

As a result of planning in this manner, New England towns have always had a unique, orderly, homogenous appearance, no matter what architectural style was in vogue when the town was built. Significantly, as Vincent Scully has pointed out, the concept of the connected row house was resisted in rural New England in favor of detached, single-family dwellings along broad and graceful tree-lined streets. Conceptually, this combination of stately trees and uniformly imposing middle-class homes was a new American creation, easily distinguished from the English farming villages and towns from which so many of the early settlers came. And visually speaking, whether the houses were covered with darkened clapboard or painted white with black shutters in later times, this unique combination of woodlands and country village has always maintained its appeal for New World eyes, especially in the autumn.

As a matter of fact, taking this idea one step further, the image of a peaceful and prosperous New England settlement—with a steeple or two rising above the surrounding autumn foliage—seems to have carried intensely patriotic associations. As one Yankee traveler put it, during a tour of Connecticut in the early fall of 1789, seeing the morning sun as it lifted "the vapors of night" from a fertile valley was like watching a rising curtain that revealed a joyful vision of "forests, spires, and cultivation"—the most symbolic features of a wilderness landscape being tamed and inhabited by Americans.

Although it may be difficult now to visualize an entire community filled with nothing but seventeenth-century buildings, the few houses that have survived from that period offer us a chance to see exactly how they were built and what they were like to live in. To begin with in the long process of erecting a new house, the foundations (marking the perimeter of the first floor) had to be brought up above ground level, while the massive chimney stack (with fireplace openings for each room) was constructed in the very center of the site. The number of rooms in a given plan depended, of course, on how much the proprietor was willing to pay. The Parson Capen House (1683) represents a typical two-room plan, while the Whitman House (1664) in Farmington, Connecticut, shows the so-called salt-box shape in which the original profile of the house was changed by the later addition of a lean-to at the back, adding two or three more rooms, but reducing the rear façade to only one story.

Once thick wooden sills had been anchored to the foundation walls of a given house, the owner, the carpenters he hired, and the neighbors who came to help could finish the job rather rapidly. The heavy oak posts and beams of the structure were "cut and framed" on the ground with a broadax and an adz. Then the prefabricated "frames" of the front and back walls were raised into place by many hands and linked together by horizontal beams, called end or chimney girts; these, in turn, were firmly secured to the vertical posts by means of wooden pins through the mortise-and-tenon joints. Smaller pieces of timber were added next at carefully spaced intervals to begin filling in the rectangular skeleton of the frame. Rafters gave shape to the high-pitched roof, which might have several cross gables as well as the one on each end; floor joists, supported in the middle by summer beams, divided the interior space into separate floors, while studs and braces began to fill in the wall areas. Finally, wood shingles served as a relatively cheap yet durable covering for the roof; sawed boards of varying widths were used for flooring over the joists; and the walls were finished with wattle-and-daub fill between the studs, protected from the New England weather on the outside by a clapboard covering.

Looking at these early colonial houses, one is always struck by the forthright honesty and simplicity of the design, and it is impossible not to read these qualities as a commentary on the directness and probity of their Puritan builders and occupants. Even though the general shape (including the overhang) and specific details (such as the casement windows and the carved pendants or drops) were derived from identifiable English prototypes, this sort of house in New England tended to be sparer and more insistently geometric or boxlike than its cousins across the Atlantic. An uncompromising, no-nonsense attitude can be seen in the way in which the clapboard sheathing is stretched across the wall plane, from corner post to corner post, like the taut paper skin of a box kite. Decorative ornament was obviously held to the barest minimum; only the carved pendants on the façade, the diamond-paned windows, and the nail-studded door with its wrought-iron hardware were permitted to play off against the horizontal rhythm of the overlapping clapboards.

In terms of coloring, the shingles and siding on many of these early homes may have been left in a natural state and allowed to darken naturally with age—until the wood began to rot away, that is, and had to be replaced every five or ten years. On the other hand, there is some evidence that a red earth pigment combined with fish oil was also used in this period—more, perhaps, as a preservative to prolong the life of the raw clapboard than as a matter of aesthetic necessity.

On the interior, these seventeenth-century houses have a characteristic look and feel. Even without period furnishings (such as simple New England chairs, chests, trestle-foot tables, and court cupboards, holding valuable pewter, plates, and accessories), the space alone would have a functional appeal, stemming from the simple room plan, the low ceilings, the small casements, and the completely honest, undisguised use of materials—heavy wood, whitewash, and stone or brick. Although the central core of each house was a massive chimney, most of the sheer bulk of the masonry could not be seen except as it emerged from the roof. Instead, it was the negative openings in this solid core, namely the large fireplaces in every room, that served as life-sustaining sources of light and heat.

Structural timbers, especially the summer beams and the joists they supported for the floor above, were left exposed. To cover them with a false ceiling would have been uselessly expensive and would have reduced the limited headroom even further. The inside walls were usually finished with a coat of plaster, but wainscoting or full paneling (especially for the fireplace wall) were also common in more expensive homes. In the seventeenth century carpets or floorcloths were rarely spread out to cover the random-width flooring; if a family was wealthy enough to own a Turkey-work carpet, it was used as a colorful table covering—much too valuable to be trod upon—following a standard European practice of the age.

On the question of interior coloring, the most recent research published by Abbott Lowell Cummings has shown that some (and, by implication, perhaps many) rooms of the period were not coated and recoated with whitewash alone, as most modern restorations would have us believe. Toward the end of the seventeenth century our Puritan ancestors seem to have grown more fond of exciting color combinations to dramatize the spaces they lived in. Careful analysis of paint layers in several surviving interiors shows that contrasting shades (such as black versus white or brown versus yellow) were applied to the exposed structural timbers, especially the central summer beam and supporting posts, to create striking visual effects. In some instances an entire room might be treated with a single distinctive color (yellow, green, or blue, for example) with upholstery on the chairs and draperies at the windows to match. Still later houses had rooms in which the wood around the fireplace, if not all the adjacent paneling, was painted in imitation marble, and in some places walls and even ceilings were covered with crude polka dots as a stylish, decorative motif.

From all appearances, therefore, including what was recorded by contemporary limners in their portrait paintings, it would seem that by 1675–1700 the original simplicity of Puritan life and the original truth-to-materials in early New England domestic architecture were beginning to succumb to the pressures of increasing affluence and materialism. Money, the inevitable product of Yankee industry and thrift, could now be conspicuously displayed in several forms. Larger houses with more elegant decorations were not the only means of expressing one's self or one's social position. In terms of clothing, first of all, the simple black garments with white collars of the early Puritan settlers were being abandoned in favor of finer and more colorful apparel —as seen in the anonymous paintings of *John Freake* and his wife *Mrs. Elizabeth Freake and Baby Mary* (Worcester Art Museum), commissioned in Boston about 1674. Even from the easel of a relatively unschooled limner, companion portraits of this sort must have been rather expensive items in themselves, making an impressive addition to the furnishings in the homes of sitters who could afford them.

More importantly, by the beginning of the eighteenth century, silver "plate," imported from England or manufactured by colonial craftsmen, was starting to replace wooden or pewter serving pieces, dinner plates, and eating utensils on more than just ceremonial occasions. Before the age of savings banks, it must have been tempting to keep bags of silver coins hidden away, but this was not a particularly safe procedure. A man's wealth in negotiable coins was far better protected by hiring a silversmith to melt the silver down and then turn the bullion into unique but functional shapes, engraved with the owner's initials and stamped with the maker's hallmark. Among the pieces one might commission from Jeremiah Dummer in 1676 or Paul Revere in 1776 were sugar bowls, saltcellars, pepper shakers, mustard pots, knives, forks, and spoons, porringers, dram cups, candle cups, tumblers, beakers, tankards, basins, monteiths, candlesticks, snuffers, coffee, tea, or chocolate pots, chafing dishes, salvers, shoe buckles, clasps, as well as snuff or tobacco boxes.

As the most visible sign of accumulated wealth in any household, the family "plate" was customarily arranged on open shelves or in an open cupboard where no visitor could fail to notice it, but this was a relatively private form of ostentation. On the ritual occasions of marriage or funeral services—particularly the latter—the richest clans could make a lavish public display of their family pride and prestige in the community.

Of all the expenses involved in burying the dead in colonial times, payment for the carving and erecting of a gravestone was obviously the most permanent manifestation of money. Each stone was intended to be an eternal marker, inscribed to the memory of an individual life, but the images used by the carver above or around the inscription also speak of the colonists' collective view of themselves in relationship to God and of their vision of life after death. That is what makes it so fascinating to wander through rural graveyards, scattered over the New England countryside, or to revisit the more densely populated burying grounds in larger settlements where the early tombstones are gathered in related clusters. Looking closely, we can see that the emotionally charged symbols of winged death's-heads, crossed bones, skeletons, and hourglasses on seventeenth-century headstones were clearly descended from medieval folk images and superstitions. An age-old fear of evil and sorcery was certainly evident in the famous Salem witch trial hysteria of 1692; in a similar way, the fearful graveyard images of the time were a grim reminder to every man, to every sinful Christian, that he had to be prepared to account for his life before the Final Judge, since the horrible specter of death might come to claim him at any moment.

Eighteenth-century tombstones in New England tended to be noticeably more optimistic, more decorative, and, one assumes, more expensive. Death's-heads became more angelic; flowers and garlands took the place of picks and shovels; rich decorative borders indicated something of the wealth of the deceased; and symbols for the sun, moon, and stars were a firm indication that the soul of the departed would surely rise to Heaven, rather than moldering in the grave or suffering endless pain and punishment in the fiery pits of Hell.

As Allan Ludwig has shown in his beautiful book *Graven Images*, a prominent funeral included more than simply burying the wooden coffin and erecting a headstone. Usually there was an entire procession, beginning at the meetinghouse, where a sermon had just been read to honor the deceased. If the family was influential enough to obtain the services of a leading divine, his eloquent words might be printed afterward—adding, of course, to the expenses incurred. The procession to the burying ground consisted of at least a horse and cart, appropriately draped in black, to carry the coffin; hired mourners, perhaps; and members of the family and friends, wearing mourning rings, cloaks, special scarfs, and gloves that were purchased expressly for this one purpose. By 1720–1722 and again in 1741–1742, sumptuary laws had to be passed in Massachusetts to prevent excessive shows of wealth at funerals because they were beginning to get out of hand, needlessly impoverishing the dead man or woman's relatives.

In any consideration of art and life in colonial America, the year 1700 always looms as an especially important date. It separates nearly a century of struggle, survival, and initial success from a new and brighter era of ever-increasing prosperity and enlightenment, leading ultimately before another century had passed to the political unrest and open warfare of the Revolution.

At the same time, 1700 conveniently serves as the most appropriate dividing line between the essentially medieval heritage of seventeenth-century arts and crafts and the arrival in the colonies of more up-to-date ideas or stylistic impulses. In the case of eighteenth-century furniture (furniture meaning all "the utensils requisite for a house or any other thing"), the terms we use for specific style periods—William and Mary (1690–1730), Queen Anne (1725–1760), and Chippendale (1755–1790)—are clearly English in origin. And the same is equally true for Colonial architecture that is universally called Georgian (or, less frequently, Wren Baroque).

These stylistic labels should make us mindful of several things. First of all, the American colonies were extraordinarily dependent on the mother country in one way or another for almost every aspect of their culture—from common laws to religious beliefs, from the simplest trades to the highly honored professions and the finer arts. Secondly, the latest styles imported from London were consistently admired, even by those who preferred the simpler pleasures or virtues of colonial life, compared to the extravagances and temptations of the English capital. And lastly, in the Northern colonies, at least, no one man could afford to emulate the example set by the richest landowners and noblemen in England; instead, it was the pattern established by the well-to-do middle-class merchants and country squires "at home" that could be followed on this side of the Atlantic.

After 1700 there was a fundamental change in the type of house a wealthy man might build for himself and his family in the vicinity of Boston or in one of the other thriving seaports along the New England coast, from Portsmouth, New Hampshire, to Newport, Rhode Island. To be sure, the earlier house type survived, especially in rural areas, but the old-fashioned elements of informal planning (lean-tos were often added by each new generation of occupants), asymmetry in the placement of doors and windows, and the insistent verticality of seventeenth-century façades and end gables were consciously discarded. In their place came a new set of design principles, stressing geometric order as well as horizontal stability and calm—with special interest given to the decorative treatment of entrances, windows, corners, and roof lines.

The Isaac Royall House in Medford, Massachusetts, represents a typical "town-house" form of the early Colonial Georgian period, a form that was copied from a type of stately row house to be found in parts of London. A desire to keep up with English precedents, even at a great distance, is certainly clear in how this particular house evolved. To begin with, in 1733–1737 the pre-existing brick house on the site was completely rebuilt and partially sheathed in wood. This new veneer consisted of clapboard and more elegant detailing in the form of wood panels between the windows, quoins at the corners (imitating stone construction), and a distinctive cornice to set off the top of the wall. The east façade of the house survives in this form.

The west façade as it exists today was added by Isaac Royall, Jr., in 1747–1750, but the basic plan was established in the 1730s when the cramped one-room depth of the original building was expanded to the more commodious arrangement called in that period a "double pile." In a typical ground plan of this type there were four rooms on the first floor—two on either side of the entryway that ran from the front to the back door.

On the exterior, the new four-room plan with central passage allowed for greater precision in the placement of expressive details. Most importantly, doors with their fashionable "broken" pediments—so often framing a pineapple ornament, the symbol of hospitality—could be centered exactly in the middle of a street or garden façade. And the windows, in turn, could then be spread out across the wall plane in a tightly controlled but rhythmical manner that must have deeply pleased both the patron and his carpenter-builder. On the inside, moreover, the central passageway (including the stairs to the second floor) was often surprisingly wide in relation to the rest of an eighteenth-century house. This open space was made possible, of course, by removing the chimney core of earlier domestic buildings and transferring the fireplaces to the outside walls at each end of the house.

A recent book issued by the Society for the Preservation of New England Antiquities contains a compilation of rural household inventories from the area around Boston in colonial times (1675–1775). At first sight such a publication might seem-suited for American antiquarians only, but the fact of the matter is that this survey permits us to understand the differences between a typical seventeenth- and a typical eighteenth-century house from the inside, as it were—from the point of view of a member of the household. In a standard central chimney and added lean-to house of the later 1600s, the two main rooms on the first floor were the *parlor* and the *hall*. In the *parlor*, as Abbott Lowell Cummings has pointed out, a family kept its finest furniture, including the best feather bed, bolsters, sheets, blankets, curtains, valances, and bedstead, for this was the parents' bedroom, in addition to serving as the proper room in which to entertain company on special occasions.

The *hall*, on the other side of the massive chimney, was unquestionably the center of family life, especially in the colder months when a fire was kept going in this room throughout the day and probably well into the evening. If there was no lean-to with a separate kitchen, then all the cooking was done in this room alone. According to surviving inventories for 1675 to 1700, food and cooking utensils could always be found in the *hall* along with the less valuable furniture, such as additional chairs, a wooden table or two, a settle, perhaps a trundle bed, and another cupboard.

In any lean-to addition the central room was the kitchen, its fireplace joined to the masonry core of the entire house. Here one would find all the necessary accessories for cooking over an open fire—iron pots and hooks, brass pots, frying pans, warming pans, skillets, skimmers, ladles, tongs, and so forth. On either side of the kitchen were smaller rooms: a buttery or dairy where milk products could be kept cool, and a snug bedroom on the warmer side. Lastly, on the second floor were two more bedrooms called the *parlor chamber* or the *hall chamber*, depending on which room was directly underneath. If the family was a large one, the children might have had to sleep in a dormitory-like arrangement of rows of beds without much other furniture. In rural areas one of these second-floor chambers might also be used for dry storage of grains and other foodstuffs. And if the owner was rich enough to own a black slave or two, there was still space under the eaves to create a garret bedroom for these family retainers.

In sharp contrast to the homely simplicity and utility of earlier plans, there is an undeniable sense of formal elegance in the symmetrical layouts of four rooms plus entry of the Georgian era. In houses of this type the uses of the various rooms were far more clearly marked out. Two of the first-floor rooms were parlors, for example. The *best parlor* contained the most expensive furnishings and was used on the most ceremonial social occasions. The inventory of the estate of the first Isaac Royall (1739) shows that the "Best Room" in his house in Medford contained —besides the side chairs, wooden tables, and standing chests that were imported or perhaps locally made—a costly "peer Looking Glass," flanked by a pair of "large Sconsces," a marble table with iron frames, a "Turkey carpitt," and a "Jappaned tea table" with "a Sett of Cheney [China] for the Same," waiting for callers. These elegant touches undoubtedly looked most impressive in eighteenth-century rooms that were higher (no exposed beams were allowed to protrude through the smooth surfaces with elegant trim) and brighter (thanks to larger sash windows with larger panes instead of casements).

The *second parlor*, it has been shown, was somewhat less well furnished, and so it was used for less important events. At times it could be used as a "dining" or "eating" room, but this usage was not a fixed purpose, by any means.

The surprisingly spacious *entry* or *entryway* through the middle of the house, being a foyer or passageway essentially, had little furniture other than a side table, chairs, and perhaps a clock. Leather bags or buckets of water were kept near the door, though, so that at the very first cry of "Fire" or the first sound of the nearest bell the men of each household could run out to join the brigade that would try to extinguish the threat to the entire community.

The entry was also the customary place for hanging a glass lantern or two in addition to pictures and prints. In seventeenth-century New England houses there was seldom anything finer on the walls than an occasional map or "papar picture" (an English engraving), and limner portraits must have been extremely rare compared to the number of dwellings in all the colonial settlements from north of Massachusetts Bay to the towns west of the Connecticut River. In the eighteenth century, however, copper-plate engravings, mezzotints, decorative maps, and even paintings on glass became common household features even in outlying districts. "Fram'd and Glaz'd" whole series of prints could be found in Georgian homes, hanging in rows upon the walls of the entry and on the paneled stairs. As to subject matter, American taste seems to have run to famous Old World views or prospects, portraits of English royalty, inoffensive allegories, copies after Raphael's cartoons (in one case, at least), and by mid-century an occasional Hogarth. A few New World subjects were available as well—such as the mezzotint portraits of the four Indian kings (Mohawk chiefs) who visited Queen Anne in 1710 or the likenesses of leading ministers in the New England area.

Original works of art, on the other hand, were naturally more expensive and rarer, but in the course of the eighteenth century the number of oil paintings to be seen in well-to-do homes increased rapidly—just as the social status of the artist improved from the level of a mere craftsman (limner or painter-stainer) to the more exalted station of a man of talent and position (John Singleton Copley), whose services were in such demand that he had to refuse commissions at times. Family portraits in their carved and gilded frames were probably hung in the best parlor but not necessarily over the mantelpiece. In the finest Georgian interiors the entire chimney breast was treated as a single decorative unit, the design of which was frequently copied almost verbatim from an English carpenter's guide or pattern book. Above the mantelpiece itself the moldings were used to create a center of visual interest for the entire room, inviting the insertion of a painting. But, since the overmantel area was square or horizontal in format, this space was more suitable for landscape or seascape paintings than for single portraits, which tended to be taller than they were wide.

In one of the larger New England towns a wealthy homeowner might go out and buy a painting already framed to hang over his front-parlor fireplace. In a rural area, though, completion of the overmantel might have to wait until an itinerant painter visited the area. When a wandering artist did arrive, he was invited into one country house after another and commissioned to paint—directly on the paneling over the mantelpiece—either a topographical portrait of the house itself or else a completely imaginary scene. Where rich city dwellers put large pots of fresh-cut flowers on the hearth to brighten up the dark chimney opening during the summer months, this practice was also imitated in the country. Rural patrons simply hired an artist to paint a pot of flowers on the chimney boards that were used to close off fireplaces that were not needed in the warmer weather.

Besides the two parlors and the entry, the other first-floor rooms in a standard eighteenth-century house were the keeping room and the kitchen. Befitting its role as a family apartment, the keeping room naturally had less expensive furniture that would stand up to hard use. A built-in open cupboard-like structure in a corner of the room held the china plates and glassware between meals, while a card table against the wall could be pulled out after dinner for a game or two. In a rural kitchen as late as 1770 one would still find such basic items as butter churns, mortars and pestles, spinning wheels, and dozen of pewter plates and utensils measured by the pound rather than by the piece, along with cider barrels, washtubs, dripping pans, earthenware plates, a kneading trough, a cheese press, damask tablecloths, any number of "diaper napkins," and an occasional mousetrap or two—all this in addition to the assortment of brass and iron pots, pans, and fireplace accessories in standard use in the colonies for a century or more. In view of the sheer quantity of items present in an eighteenth-century kitchen, without the impressive organization provided by rows of nails, hooks, open shelves, and drawers it might have become impossible to find the right tool at the right time while cooking. And the problem of moving about while preparing a meal could be solved only by keeping strict order among the larger pieces of furniture, such as the wooden table, the straw-bottom chairs, the settle by the fire, and all the assorted boxes, chests, casks, kegs, and similar containers that were needed for storage.

Firearms are mentioned in several of the pre-1775 household inventories that have been published for eastern Massachusetts. A rich city dweller might keep ceremonial armor in the entryway of his house in Dorchester or Boston, but in the country a gun with a bayonet and a powder horn could be found hanging from hooks either in the keeping room or in the kitchen. No longer needed for defense against the Indians, these were the guns that could be grabbed at a moment's notice by Minutemen willing to defend their rights and their liberty against the British troops who marched on Lexington and Concord.

The upstairs bedchambers in a colonial house of the 1700s were often rather beautifully appointed—with an over-all color scheme strongly at work from the bedclothes (sometimes in crewel work) to the curtains, from the chair coverings to the coat of paint or the imported decorative paper on the walls. Scholars in the field of American furniture have shown that colonial bedrooms contained—besides the bedstead and its trappings—chests of drawers and easy chairs that were seldom or never found below stairs. Although highboys or lowboys do appear in some restored parlors open to the public, this is allowed more for the sake of illustrating a period style in cabinetmaking than for demonstrating correct usage. While the largest and most massive pieces of first-floor furniture were secretaries and desks, even the most exquisitely finished American Chippendale highboys were apparently used upstairs—for storing clothes and linen—in the master bedroom. Similarly, lowboys served as dressing tables with drawers below for storage. And finally, the easy chair was almost exclusively the province of the elderly and the infirm, who kept to their chambers most of the day. The wings on such a fully upholstered chair served as a healthy, built-in protection again too much heat radiating from the fireplace or too much cold air from the inevitable drafts. In colonial portraiture we find that the easy chair did indeed have special associations. In Copley's work, for example, it was only older women—grandmothers, in fact—who willingly posed for their portraits surrounded by the easy chairs that supported and protected them through months of illness or years of old age.

If the east façade of the Isaac Royall House in Medford can be taken to represent the early Georgian style in domestic architecture in the Northern colonies, then the Jeremiah Lee Mansion of 1768 in Marblehead, Massachusetts, is certainly the paradigm of later Georgian town-house design—marked by a grander scale and far greater pretensions. What sort of man built this monumental block is evident even on the exterior. With its three-story height (accented by the cupola in the middle of the roof) and its impressive horizontal bulk, set close to the street, the house makes an unmistakable impression of wealth and power.

Compared to earlier eighteenth-century homes, the Lee Mansion (1768) exhibits a degree of aggressiveness that must be read as a reflection of rising prosperity in the colonies before the Revolution. The central part of the street façade, for instance, asserts itself by projecting forward slightly, capped by its own pediment. And the main door to the street now has an entrance portico with self-consciously correct Classical details, setting a trend for others to follow.

Aside from these projections, however, the overriding impulse of the Lee Mansion remains decidedly horizontal and earthbound. The over-all width of the façade is stressed by horizontal lines—lines formed by the modillioned cornice, the rows of windows, and the joints in what appears to be rusticated masonry. In reality, though, the entire surface of this building is made of wood—the New England material, par excellence. Even the quoins at the corners of the structure, so clearly marked in a contrasting color, are wood rather than the stone blocks they pretend to be.

On the interior the Jeremiah Lee Mansion was, if anything, even more ostentatious. In the major rooms extravagant veneers and surface decorations again were used to reflect the owner's mercantile success. One of the first-floor parlors, for example, was completely paneled in one material (relatively inexpensive American pine) and then painstakingly painted to simulate the color and graining of more costly woodwork (dark English oak). Wherever possible, sumptuous refinements, such as Sadler tiles or colorful wallpapers, were imported from England to finish the interior with as much style and sophistication as possible for this side of the North Atlantic. When imported stuffs and accessories were not immediately available, a man as rich as Jeremiah Lee could hire the services of the finest local craftsmen who, in their own provincial way, tried to imitate the latest fashions in English interiors and furnishings.

Perhaps the clearest visual record of Jeremiah Lee's vigorous and confident self-image as a man of property can be found in the pair of paintings he commissioned from the leading painter in the colonies, John Singleton Copley. Not content with half-length or even three-quarter-length pictures, Lee had to have life-size, standing portraits of himself and his wife in idealized settings to hang on the gorgeous walls of his new house.

In his significant study of *American Buildings and Their Architects; The Colonial and Neoclassical Styles*, William H. Pierson, Jr., has identified a key problem with respect to the Colonial Georgian style. Using the Lee Mansion as a prime example, Pierson points out that the aggressive nature of successful American merchants often shines through in the design of their homes; at the same time, though, the more refined Classical details of a house like the Lee Mansion may also mirror the owner's fundamental wish to be a cultured English gentleman with elevated tastes. We must realize, therefore, that what we often admire as the highest achievements of Colonial domestic architecture were built by the richest magnates who thought of themselves as Englishmen, not as Americans.

This problem has political overtones, as well, since many of the wealthy property owners in the colonies were Loyalists or Tories. According to a contemporary definition, "In America, the word Tory now implies *a friend to the supremacy of the British constitution over all the empire*; and the word Whig, *an asserter of colonial independence*, or (what is just the same) of legislations distinct and divided from British legislation, in all the several provinces." While the Tory merchants tried to maintain the *status quo* that was good for their businesses and good for their comfortable private lives, it was the radical, dissident, Whig-led rabble in the streets who demanded change. Frequently they demanded it so violently that leading loyalists fled the colonies for the safety of London, leaving their luxurious homes to be captured like symbolic prizes in an ideological war against the British government.

It goes almost without saying that of all the provinces along the coast of North America it was Massachusetts which led the fight against the Stamp Act, against the quartering of English soldiers, and against other arbitrary impositions of British rule. In the words of Israel Mauduit, at the opening of his history of the New England colonies, "In all the late *American* Disturbances, and in every Attempt against the Authority of the *British* Government, the People of *Massachusetts Bay* have taken the Lead. Every new Move towards Independence has been theirs: And in every fresh Mode of Resistance against the Laws, they have first set the Example, and then issued their admonitory Letters to the other Colonies to follow it."

Boston was, of course, the natural epicenter of the resistance movement in Massachusetts where the most dramatic and often violent clashes or confrontations took place before the actual opening of armed hostilities in April 1775. In retrospect it is fascinating to see how contemporary eyewitness accounts of the city of Boston changed from the 1630s to the 1770s as public interest shifted from material development (progress) to political problems.

To William Wood in 1634, as quoted above, the site of the future city was little more than a rocky neck of land with little timber or grazing land for cattle. When John Josselyn arrived at Boston in July 1638, he came ashore in a small boat to pay his respects to Governor Winthrop; the settlement "then was rather a Village, than a Town, there being not above Twenty or Thirty houses," and he remembered "being civilly treated by all [he] had occasion to converse with." On a second visit in 1663, Boston made a much stronger impression on Josselyn. He described it then as "the Metropolis of this Colony, or rather of the whole Countrey, situated upon a Peninsula, about four miles in compass, almost square, and invironed with the Sea, saving one small Isthmus which gives access to other Towns by land on the South-side. . . . The houses are for the most part raised on the Sea-banks and wharfed out with great industry and cost, many of them standing upon piles, close together on each side of the streets as in London, and furnished with many fair shops. . . . With three meeting Houses or Churches, and a Town-house built upon pillars where the Merchants may confer; in the Chambers above they keep their monthly Courts. Their streets are many and large, paved with pebble stone, and the south-side adorned with Gardens and Orchards."

By the time of John Oldmixon's inventory of *The British Empire in America*, published in 1708, Boston had grown to ten or twelve thousand souls, making it larger than Exeter, England, and certainly "the biggest City in America, except two or three on the Spanish Continent." Furthermore, the town of Boston enjoyed an "abundance of fine buildings in it, publick and private," while serving as the chief port of the colony, whence "3 or 400 Sail of Ships have been loaden a Year, with Lumber, Fish, Beef, Pork, &c., for several parts of *Europe* and *America*."

During more than a century of Boston's existence as the capital of Massachusetts Bay there had been a number of armed conflicts involving the colony as a whole. But in all the various wars, from the extermination of the belligerent Pequots in 1637 to the end of the French and Indian War (1754–1763), it had never been necessary for volunteers to fight in the streets of Boston itself. In 1765, however, the attempt to enforce the Stamp Act passed by the British

Parliament precipitated riots in many places, especially Boston, where the mansion of Lieutenant Governor Thomas Hutchinson was sacked and burned in protest. Although the Stamp Act was repealed the following year, other sources of irritation continued to cause trouble.

After the violent incident of the Boston Massacre on March 5, 1770, nothing could have been further from the minds of liberal leaders, such as James Otis and Samuel Adams, than publishing the kind of peaceful, idyllic description of their city that had been so popular twenty-five, fifty, or a hundred years earlier. What they wanted instead was the most accurate information obtainable under oath, information with which they could indict the British soldiers involved and their commanding officer as ruthless murderers. The following is but one of many sworn statements published in *A Short Narrative of the Horrid Massacre in Boston*, a pamphlet that was printed by order of the Town:

[Deposition No. 44]

I, Charles Hobby, of lawful age, testify and say, that on Monday evening the 5th [of March], between the hours of nine and ten o'clock, being in my master's house, was alarmed with the cry of fire. I ran down as far as the town-house, and then heard that the soldiers and the inhabitants were fighting in the alley of Dr. Cooper's meeting-house. I went through the alley, I there saw a number of soldiers about the barracks, some with muskets, others without. I saw a number of officers at the door of the mess-house, almost fronting the alley, and some of the inhabitants intreating the officers to command the soldiers to be peaceable and retire to their barracks. One of the officers, viz., Lieut. Minchin, replied, that the soldiers had been abused lately by the inhabitants, and that if the inhabitants would disperse, the soldiers should follow their example. Captain Goldfinch was among the rest of the officers in or about the steps of the mess-house door, but did not command the soldiers.

I then left them and went to King Street. I then saw a party of soldiers loading their muskets about the Custom-house door, after which they all shouldered. I heard some of the inhabitants cry out, "Heave no snow balls!"; others cried, "They dare not fire!" Capt. Preston was then standing by the soldiers, when a snowball struck a grenadier, who immediately fired, Capt. Preston standing close by him. The Captain then spoke distinctly, "Fire, Fire!" I was then within four feet of Captain Preston, and know him well; the soldiers fired as fast as they could one after another. I saw the mulatto [Crispus Attucks] fall, and Mr. Samuel Gray went to look at him. One of the soldiers at a distance of about four or five yards, pointed his piece directly for the said Gray's head and fired. Mr. Gray, after struggling, turned himself right round upon his heel and fell dead. Capt. Preston some time after ordered [the soldiers] to march to the guard-house. I then took up a round hat and followed the people that carried [Mr. Gray] down to a house near the post-office.

—Boston, March 20, 1770.

On the eve of the Revolution, political agitation and turmoil in the streets of Boston must have seemed almost endless—especially in the opinion of the Tories, who had such an enormous vested interested in conserving the social and political system that supported their status as the ruling class. Their arch enemies in the propaganda battle for the public's sympathy were the

Whig politicians, the radical orators, and the clever pamphleteers who could fan the slightest friction into raging flames.

According to one apologist for the conservative viewpoint who wrote a series of letters to the Boston newspapers in 1774–1775 under the pseudonym of Massachusettensis, the rhetorical combat between the Whigs and the Tories was inherently unequal. The Whigs had a great initial advantage because "their scheme flattered the people with the idea of independence [whereas] the Tories' plan supposed a degree of subordination, which is rather an humiliating idea; besides there is a propensity in men to believe themselves injured and oppressed whenever they are told so."

In one of his long letters to the editor (December 19, 1774), reprinted by a sympathetic Boston publisher in 1776, Massachusettensis attempted to counterindict the tactics of the Whigs by making them look silly, irresponsible, or sinister. Rereading this letter today, however, offers us a glimpse of what was happening in the streets below the writer's windows together with a better idea of how many grievances the Tories were willing to play down or simply overlook in the hope of keeping the peace between the colonies and the mother country:

> The ferment, raised in their minds in the time of the stamp-act, was not yet allayed, and the leaders of the whigs had gained the confidence of the people by their successes in their former struggle; so they had nothing to do but to keep up the spirit among the people, and they were sure of commanding this province. . . .
>
> They accordingly applied themselves to work upon the imagination, and to inflame the passion; for this work they possessed great talents. I will do justice to their ingenuity. They were intimately acquainted with the feelings of man, and knew all the avenues to the human heart:—Effigies, paintings, and other imagery, were exhibited; the fourteenth of August was celebrated annually as a festival in commemoration of a mob's destroying a building, owned by the late Lieutenant Governor [Thomas Hutchinson], which was supposed to have been erected for a stamp-office, and compelling him to resign his office of stamp-master under liberty-tree [the famous elm on Washington Street, Boston]; annual orations were delivered in the old-south meeting house, on the fifth of March, the day when some persons were unfortunately killed by a party of the twenty-ninth regiment; lists of imaginary grievances were continually published; the people were told weekly, that the ministry had formed a plan to enslave them; that the duty upon tea was only a prelude to a window-tax, hearth-tax, land-tax, and poll-tax, and these were only paving the way for reducing the country to lordships; this bait was the more easily swallowed, as there seems to be an apprehension of that kind hereditary to the people of New-England; and they were conjured by the duty they owed themselves, their country, and their GOD, by the reverence due to the sacred memory of their ancestors, and all their toils and sufferings in this once inhospitable wilderness, and by their affections for unborn millions, to rouse and exert themselves in the common cause.

Only four months after this letter was written, the "common cause" turned into open rebellion.

Fireplace in the kitchen of the Buttolph–Williams House.

The Buttolph–Williams House, Old Wethersfield, Connecticut, built about 1690.

OPPOSITE: Rare twin high chairs and an unusual seventeenth-century settle in the kitchen of the Buttolph–Williams House.

Kitchen utensils from the Buttolph–Williams House.

The Whitman House, Farmington, Connecticut, 1664. The six-inch gabled overhang and carved pendants are classic features of the early New England style. The lean-to at the rear was added shortly after 1700.

OPPOSITE: A corner pendant on the Whitman House.

Diamond-pane windows of the Whitman House.

OVERLEAF: The Whipple House, c. 1640, Ipswich, Massachusetts, grew with the generations. Originally it had one room; in 1670 Captain John Whipple built an addition that more than doubled its size. The third owner, Major John Whipple, added a rear lean-to.

The Sergeant John Deming House, c. 1666–1667, Wethersfield, Connecticut, a good example of early lean-to construction.

OPPOSITE, BELOW: The Old Dustin Garrison House, erected by Thomas Dustin at Haverhill, Massachusetts, in 1697. Colonists lived in great fear of the Indians, a concern crystallized by King Philip's War in 1675. "Blockhouse" and "garrison" are often used interchangeably, although "blockhouse" more narrowly meant a square fort with overhangs.

ABOVE: White Horse Tavern, Newport, Rhode Island, c. 1673.

An early type of trunk carved from a tree bole is in the Old Ordinary Inn, Hingham, Massachusetts. The bonnets are nineteenth century.

OVERLEAF: The Thomas Lee House, East Lyme, Connecticut, was constructed in 1664. The lean-to was added later.

The Parson Capen House, built for the Reverend Joseph Capen at Topsfield, Massachusetts, in 1683, is considered one of the perfect New England colonial houses, even though the restoration was not always faithful to the original. Front and gable overhangs and pilastered chimneys reflect the English Tudor heritage.

OPPOSITE: Place setting from the Old Ordinary Inn in Hingham. The wooden plate is more than three hundred years old.

A bedchamber in the Richard Jackson house, c. 1684, Portsmouth, New Hampshire. The wide floor boards are typical of the period.

OPPOSITE: Doorway of the Wanton–Lyman–Hazard House, Newport, Rhode Island.

RIGHT: The Nancy Murphy House, c. 1725, at 35 Washington Street on the point in Newport, has been restored to its original appearance by the Newport Restoration Foundation. In contrast to the residences of wealthy merchants it is small and bare of decoration.

BELOW: The Wanton–Lyman–Hazard House, 1675, is the oldest standing house in Newport, and one of the finest Jacobean houses in New England.

OVERLEAF: A room with seventeenth-century furniture from the Hunter House, Newport (page 63).

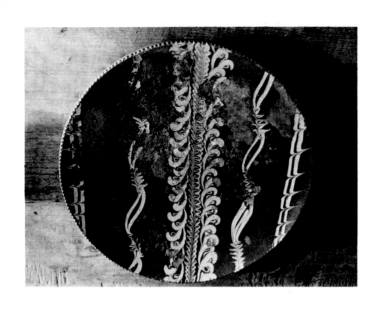

LEFT, ABOVE: Slipware was one of the earliest types of pottery used in the colonies. This plate from the Judson House in Stratford, Connecticut, is characteristic of the eighteenth century.

LEFT: Detail of the kitchen of the Wanton–Lyman–Hazard House (page 47).

ABOVE: An interior view of the oldest part of the Abraham Browne House in Watertown, Massachusetts, built about 1698. The bed, covered by crewel bedcovers, dates from 1674. A Persian rug covers the table, and the chairs are in the English Jacobean style.

RIGHT: Algonquian Indian mortar and pestle in the Judson House in Stratford, Connecticut.

Portrait of Samuel Warner (1732–1771), painted by Joseph Blackburn, from the Macphaedris–Warner House in Portsmouth, New Hampshire.

The William and Mary parlor in the Winterthur Museum came from the Thomas Goble House in Lincoln, Massachusetts. Painted decoration, very popular during the William and Mary period (1690–1730), is seen here in marbleized woodwork in gray, red, and white.

OPPOSITE: A parlor from the Wentworth-Coolidge Mansion, c. 1725, Portsmouth, New Hampshire, with mid-eighteenth-century French wallpaper. This was the official residence of Benning Wentworth, first governor of the separate province of New Hampshire from 1741 to 1766, when Portsmouth was at its height of wealth and fashion.

Early Bible belonging to Historic Deerfield, Deerfield Massachusetts. Printed in England, it served as the official register of the Sheldon family.

Early Bible Box in Historic Deerfield.

BELOW: The Parson Williams House, c. 1750, today belongs to Deerfield Academy.

BELOW: The Parson Williams House, c. 1750, today belongs to Deerfield Academy.

OPPOSITE: The Frary House in Deerfield, built about 1750, was turned into a tavern in the 1760s, and a south wing was added with more kitchens, bar rooms, and a ballroom.

OVERLEAF: The broken pediment above the doorway at the Hunter House (page 63) includes a pineapple, symbol of hospitality.

56

In 1732 Isaac Royall bought a seventeenth-century brick house in Medford, Massachusetts, that was two-and-a-half stories high and only one room deep. Between 1733 and 1737 he raised the height to three stories and recased the old brick walls with clapboard. In 1739 Isaac Royall, Jr., inherited the house and more than doubled its depth, extended the end walls, and built twin chimneys, connected by parapets, at either end. This east façade dates from the first remodeling. On the west façade (1747–1750), the wood is made to imitate stone.

A shell-carved secretary in the Hunter House was probably made by John Goddard, the Newport cabinet maker, between 1750 and 1770.

OPPOSITE: Carved details of the stairway at the Hunter House indicate the employment of exceptional craftsmen.

A corner of the parlor in the Hunter House.

OPPOSITE, ABOVE: The Redwood Library in Newport, incorporated in 1747, was built by Peter Harrison in 1750. The building has been enlarged three times.

OPPOSITE, BELOW: The Vernon House, 1758, was one of the fine residences of colonial Newport.

ABOVE: Built in 1748, when Newport was a larger seaport than Boston or New York, the Hunter House reflects the prosperity of the times.

Built in 1763 by a small congregation under the leadership of Rabbi Isaac Touro, this oldest synagogue in the United States was designed by Peter Harrison, a gentleman architect.

OPPOSITE: The interior of Touro Synagogue in Newport is laid out in the traditional Sephardic manner, with a small interior and seats only around the perimeter. A gallery reserved for women is on three sides. Twelve columns represent the twelve tribes of Israel.

Early Rhode Island tombstone.

Chair made in Milford, Connecticut, about 1750, and now in the Judson House, Stratford.

ABOVE: Stairway from the Christopher Townsend House in Newport, carved by Mr. Townsend himself, an example of the eighteenth-century craftsmanship for which Newport was noted.

Stair detail from the Isaac Royall House in Medford, Massachusetts.

The Old Market Building in Newport was built in 1762 by Peter Harrison.

OVERLEAF: Buckman Tavern in Lexington, Massachusetts.

ABOVE: Sewing basket from the Derby House.

OPPOSITE: A portable desk of a type often used on ships rests on a butterfly table in the Derby House, Salem, Massachusetts.

RIGHT: Door handle and knocker from the Derby House (1762).

LEFT: The Moffat–Ladd House, Portsmouth, New Hampshire, overlooking the Piscataqua River. Built about 1763 by Captain John Moffat for his son Samuel, it reflects the prosperity of a successful mercantile family.

OPPOSITE: The kitchen in the Moffat–Ladd House.

An eighteenth-century waffle iron from the Moffat–Ladd House.

One of the largest of the pre-Revolutionary mansions, the Jeremiah Lee House (1768) in Marblehead, Massachusetts, was built on a grandiose scale.

A pre-Revolutionary tin doll in the Lee Mansion.

OPPOSITE, LEFT: Fireplace tiles from the Lee Mansion designed by John Sadler and manufactured in Liverpool in 1760.

OPPOSITE, RIGHT: Chippendale bombé chest found in the Lee Mansion, made in America c. 1760.

OPPOSITE: Congregational Church, 1771, Farmington, Connecticut.

Tombstones from a cemetery in Bolton, Connecticut.

American Jacobean press cupboard, made in the Boston area in the last quarter of the seventeenth century, in the collection of the Concord Historical Society, Concord, Massachusetts.

The master bedchamber of the Old Gaol in York, Maine.

OPPOSITE: Toy covered wagon, c. 1776, from the Emerson–Wilcox House, York, Maine.

Bathtub, hewn from a mahogany log between 1758 and 1776, in the John Paul Jones House in Portsmouth, New Hampshire.

II

THE MIDDLE COLONIES

Beyond the topographical and climatic changes that one might naturally expect to encounter in moving from one geographical area to another, travelers in the American colonies also found distinct regional differences in settlement (social system) and building (life-style) patterns as they moved south along the Atlantic coast. To be sure, many of these noticeable cultural differences may have been much more pronounced in the seventeenth century than they were in the eighteenth, but the important thing is that they remained visible. In the middle colonies, particularly, the crucible concept of America as a melting pot—where various groups of immigrants would quickly fuse into an integrated, homogenous whole—was openly contradicted by the evidence of Dutch, Swedish, English, and German settlements that retained some of their distinctive characteristics well into the modern era.

Colonial New England, as the name of the area implied, was settled and inhabited almost entirely by Englishmen. Minority groups, such as Christianized Indians, imported African slaves, or non-Puritan indentured servants (poor whites who paid for their passage to the New World by contracting to work without pay for a period of years), were never numerous enough to have much effect on the outward appearances of the dominant, middle-class, *English* culture around them. It was the well-to-do Tories, of course, not to mention the wealthy, often Anglican, colonial administrators serving the Crown, who set the highest standards in terms of stylish clothes, houses, and furnishings. Nevertheless, the political events of the 1760s and 1770s, leading up to the Revolution, clearly showed that this fashionable upper class in New England was

81

Old North Bridge, Concord.

deeply distrusted by the common people, who harbored an innate, hereditary fear of *lordships* and all their elegant trappings.

By contrast, it is possible to tell from the original territorial names of New Sweden, New Netherlands, and Penn's "Woods" that the middle colonies were decidedly multinational in origin from the start and not exclusively Anglo-Saxon. This fact, in turn, led to the obvious differences in cultural patterns. In the New Netherlands, for example, while the Dutch West India Company was extracting its profit from the lucrative fur trade, corporate control of the Hudson Valley encouraged the creation of a social system easily distinguished from New England settlements to the east (Connecticut) and the northeast (Massachusetts).

Along the fertile banks of the Hudson River, especially in the area of Fort Orange, which was renamed Albany by the British, grants of land, often in huge amounts, were given to wealthy individuals or patroons and not to groups of proprietors who had pooled their resources. In New England a new town usually involved a limited area of only about six square miles or so under community jurisdiction, but a typical grant from the West India Company involved sixteen miles of river frontage (with all the land running back from there), exclusive hunting and fishing rights (once local Indian claims had been paid off), and monopolistic control over commerce—all this placed in the hands of anyone rich or daring enough to bring fifty colonists into the region. In Rensselaerwyck, across from Albany, as in other patroonships, the tenant farmers were required to surrender at least a third of their annual harvests to the patroon or his agents in return for their initial ocean passage, the raw materials for building a house and a barn, and the necessary tools for farming. Needless to say, this patrician system of land ownership effectively discouraged the growth of a rural middle class.

In his provocative study of *Images of American Living; Four Centuries of Architecture and Furniture as Cultural Expression*, Alan Gowans has very convincingly demonstrated the social implications of stone-versus-brick construction and urban-versus-rural house types in the New Netherlands. Where colonists of other nationalities thought of stone as the most desirable material for a house—even to the point of imitating masonry construction in wood when they could not afford the real thing—the Dutch clearly preferred brick. In the early 1660s, when Pieter Bronck built a house for his family in West Coxsackie, twenty miles south of Albany, he had to use fieldstone, but in the late 1730s, when his son Leendert added a new house next to the old one, its walls were brick, carefully laid and showing the signs of skilled craftsmanship in distinctively Dutch details such as the "mouse-tooth" patterns on the gable ends. Since brick was associated in Dutch minds with the finer houses of prosperous merchants and businessmen in old as well as New Amsterdam, it is no wonder that the most successful landowners along the Hudson wanted large brick homes for themselves as symbols of their station in the world.

In the more isolated areas of the New Netherlands, however, brick dwellings, reproducing an urban pattern, were undoubtedly outnumbered by frame structures for the poorest tenants and stone houses for the small farmers. While a limited number of Dutch colonial interiors have been saved from complete destruction and preserved as period room installations in various American museums, only a handful of rural stone houses have survived (more or less intact) on their original sites. The Abraham Hasbrouck House, begun in the 1690s at New Paltz, New York, is one of these, and it begs to be compared with a rural New England house type, such as the Whitman House in Farmington, Connecticut. Clearly visible on the exterior of the Hasbrouck House are the characteristic local features of long, low, single-story fieldstone walls, arbitrarily placed windows and "Dutch doors," and a broad roof that, elsewhere in the New Netherlands, might have several small dormers and a pronounced outward flare over the eaves.

As to their interior arrangements, Gowans and other scholars have identified the "standard plan" for these rural houses built by the Dutch (as well as Huguenot and Walloon immigrants) from the seventeenth well into the eighteenth century. To begin with, a typical stone house was only one room deep; its length was created by placing three rooms side by side—a kitchen, bedroom, and parlor—each with its own fireplace (hence the several chimneys that project through the roof at irregular intervals). Other rooms, if needed, could be added later at the back.

Of the three major interior areas, easily the most interesting and culturally distinctive space must have been the bedroom. Here one would see furniture forms of a different style, stemming from different European precedents, when compared with similar pieces in New England homes. In any respectable house in the Hudson Valley, the owner's bedroom would not be complete without a *kas*, a large two-door cupboard that dominated the space. If Chippendale highboys and chest-on-chests represented the acme of colonial style in furniture-making, as practiced in Boston, Newport, and especially Philadelphia, then the rural *kases* of New York and New Jersey (or their Germanic cousins in upstate Pennsylvania) betrayed a strong degree of folk-art simplification of form under the exuberant surfaces. In the Hudson Valley examples it is clear that Dutch taste in *kases*, as in other household arts, favored massive, stocky proportions and heavy details, such as projecting cornices and bulbous "bun" feet that protruded in the front. What is more, Dutch patrons also seemed to prefer bold surface treatment on their storage cupboards, either in the form of decorative geometric designs in the joinery or else in overall trompe-l'oeil painting in grisaille, showing swags or festoons of flowers and fruits (traditional symbols of fertility) in imaginary niches.

The other imposing item of Dutch bedroom furniture was the bed itself. Where New England bedsteads had simple canopies or surrounding draperies hung from the ceiling, Dutch beds tended to be much more fully enclosed with curtains, if not actually built-in as an alcove bed, which provided the maximum amount of warmth and protection from drafts, plus the added convenience of additional storage space underneath the platform and mattress.

Given the rapidity with which urban environments have changed over the past three hundred years, it is extremely difficult now to form an adequate mental picture of what early Dutch urban settlements were like in the seventeenth century. Little remains of outlying towns such as

Fort Casimir or New Amstel (New Castle), which flourished briefly as a port on the Delaware River, first under Dutch, then Swedish (1653–1655), Dutch again, and finally British rule (after 1664). With regard to the largest town and capital of the Dutch colony, moreover, we are forced to depend on written descriptions together with a few maps and prints for a picture of what New Amsterdam was like when Peter Stuyvesant was governor (from 1647 to 1664).

From all accounts, when the Dutch West India Company established the first permanent community at the southern tip of Manhattan Island in 1625, a fort was staked out and the land was divided into building lots, streets, and boweries (farms). The earliest engraved view of New Amsterdam, published in Holland the following year, showed thirty or more houses already built, a windmill in working order, and a five-bastioned fort for security; however, much of this may have been wishful thinking—propaganda for home consumption. By the nature of its purpose as a company town, profit came before comfort in New Amsterdam. The needs of the fur trade were the first ones to be met. A stone structure thatched with reed served as a counting-house for the port; a row of five stone houses built by the company could be rented out on the first floor and reserved on the second and third for warehouse or working space; and several windmills, grinding grain into flour or sawing tree trunks into usable boards and planks, made money as a result of local demands, somewhat as an afterthought.

As of 1628, only about 270 people inhabited the new town. And, according to the earliest visitors, most of them lived not in ordinary houses but in crude temporary shelters that consisted of a hole dug into the ground, lined with planks and bark and then covered over with beams and a roof of bark or sod. Small, one-story frame dwellings followed in a few years, but these too were insubstantial—and their plank chimneys (with mud or mortar linings) and thatched roofs represented a constant fire hazard. On the other hand, bricks could be made from local materials, and lime (for mortar) was available in the form of abundant oyster shells. By the time the Dutch settlement was allowed to have its own civil government (1653), the infant city was beginning to take on a more crowded and more convincing Old World appearance, surrounded on three sides by water and protected on the north by a defensive palisade across the island (Wall Street) to protect the settlers from Indians and Englishmen.

When the English captured New Amsterdam without bloodshed in 1664, it was observed that the "severall sorts of Trades-men and merchants and mariners" who lived there had created a partial replica of the commercial and shipping centers they came from. As in Amsterdam itself, the streets and waterfronts were lined with large brick houses turned end-on to the thorough-fare as a way of saving space. The steep roofs of these prosperous houses, their stepped gable ends in brick, and ornamental flourishes in the way of initials or numerals as wrought-iron beam anchors, must have seemed terribly old-fashioned, if not downright medieval, to the English colonists who brought more up-to-date ideas to New York. The new churches, public buildings, and private homes built above Wall Street in the later seventeenth and early eighteenth centuries strongly reflected the change in political administration of the colony, but some Dutchmen were not immediately willing to surrender their national heritage just because legal jurisdiction over the land had changed hands.

It goes without saying, perhaps, that resistance to cultural change was directly proportional to distance from the trend-setting centers. Close to the ciy of New York, for example, the Dutch proprietors of extensive estates (like Philipsburg Manor or Van Cortlandt Manor) began to adopt elements of English style sometimes in the first generation or certainly in the second under British rule. Much farther out in the country, however, buildings such as Leendert Bronck's house of the late 1730s remind us that the brick town-house ideal was still alive in the minds of wealthy, conservative, rural farmers who wanted to maintain their Dutch traditions.

In spite of English dominion, then, the dogged survival of some aspects of Dutch colonial culture distinguished New York and parts of New Jersey from the other American states at the time of the Revolution, giving it a distinctive flavor. In the early nineteenth century, though, as the country homesteads along the Hudson began to disappear almost as rapidly as the old brick houses of lower Manhattan, segments of Knickerbocker history and Dutch folklore were preserved by our Romantic writers. Thanks to Washington Irving in particular, the exploits of a comic Peter Stuyvesant, the dramatic interaction of Sleepy Hollow characters (from Ichabod Crane to the Headless Horseman), and the legend of Rip Van Winkle became national stories, enjoyed by Americans of all ages. In the twentieth century, moreover, restoration groups have saved as much as possible of Dutch heritage, in spite of soaring land values; and the excavation for each new skyscraper in the financial district of New York seems to unearth, however briefly, the foundations of still another seventeenth-century building—providing further archaeological clues to what it was like when residents of Manhattan spoke only Dutch, when money was counted in guilders, and when the large City Tavern doubled as the Town Hall (Stadthuys).

If the Dutch colony was rather firmly planted, striking deep roots in the rich soil of the New World, then the Swedish settlements along the Delaware River were considerably less substantial. At first (1638), New Sweden consisted mainly of a fort at the mouth of Christina Creek, with a village in its lee which was later to become Wilmington. Efforts to expand this colony included annexation of the Dutch outpost, Fort Casimir, in 1653, but this threat to the Dutch West India Company's commercial interests on the Delaware was soon scotched by a return invasion (600 men under Peter Stuyvesant), launched from New Amsterdam. Overwhelmed by this small army, New Sweden ceased to exist as a separate entity in 1655. Political control passed to England after 1664, and claim to the so-called Three Lower Counties of what is now Delaware was transferred to William Penn in 1682.

Through all these changes, including a short period of Dutch reconquest in 1673–1674, the Swedish, Finnish, and Dutch settlers along the river above where it widens into Delaware Bay lived in relative calm. In this atmosphere they were free to build according to national patterns. The Dutch, inevitably, brought brick construction, while the Scandavanians brought a new means of erecting cheap and relatively permanent dwellings out of tree trunks, piled one on top of another, notched at the corners for interlocking strength, and caulked with mud to keep the wind out. It was the log cabin, of course—as countless writers have shown—that became the standard house type on the American frontier once the colonies had achieved independence and the growing population, hungry for land, pushed through the Appalachian Mountains to reach the fertile valleys and plains beyond.

Ultimately the log cabin, first introduced along the Delaware, became a telling symbol of frontier life and westward expansion. Where cultured English or Anglo-American travelers of the later eighteenth century considered log cabins to be crude and ugly dwellings, unpleasant to look at and uncomfortable (or worse) to live in for anyone used to a modicum of comfort, in only fifty years these same structures came to represent a new American ideal—the rugged frontier spirit—diametrically opposed to the wealthy, effete, self-indulgent society along the East Coast. In the mid-nineteenth century, furthermore, having been born in or merely associated with a log cabin was a definite asset in the political careers of men like William Henry Harrison and Abraham Lincoln. In this change we can see a deliberate switch from the Europe-oriented emulation of colonial minds to the search for other patterns and ideas, emblematic of America's new status as an emerging nation.

The other significant Swedish contribution to life in the middle colonies belonged more to the spiritual than the material realm. Several scholars have remarked that, in sharp contrast to the mercantile Dutch, the Swedish Crown (from Queen Christina to Gustavus III in the late eighteenth century) supported the colonial churches of its former subjects long after political control over their affairs was lost. The building, perhaps by Scandanavian craftsmen, of the *Old Swedes'* churches, Holy Trinity in Wilmington (1698–1699) and Gloria Dei in Philadelphia (1698–1700), are an example of continuing culture support through official channels that permitted Swedish settlers to maintain a sense of community even in the midst of English-speaking towns.

Another instance of religious and family ties between the mother country and the Swedish congregations on the Delaware is worth mentioning, especially since it brought one of the first professionally trained painters to the colonies. The artist, Gustavus Hesselius, came from a family of ministers and intellectuals; in 1711 he left Stockholm in the company of his brother, Andreas, who was being sent out as the new pastor for the Swedish church at Fort Christina. The first stop on this trip to the New World was in England, where the two brothers spent some time in London, seeing their cousin, Emanuel Swedenborg, and visiting William Penn, who gave them passports and letters of introduction for use in territories under his proprietorship.

Finally, after a long voyage across the Atlantic, the Swedish travelers arrived at their destination on May 1, 1712. Andreas, no doubt, settled down immediately to his pastoral duties, duties that he performed faithfully for a period of eleven years before returning to Sweden in 1723. Gustavus Hesselius, meanwhile, divided his time between Maryland, the settlements on the

Delaware, and Pennsylvania, always in search of commissions for whatever work he could find, from portraiture to house painting. The itinerant life may have been taxing at times, but unlike his brother, he chose to remain in America. He was, after all, the major painter for the entire region. By 1734 he was permanently established in Philadelphia with his family, and about that time he is reported to have painted most of the woodwork in the new State House (Independence Hall), as well as two famous portraits of Delaware Indian chiefs who had come to the city in the process of negotiating the sale of more of their land to the whites. Still later in his eventful life Hesselius relinquished the portrait business to his son, John, and concentrated instead on building organs and other instruments to meet the demand for church music in the German communities now known as Pennsylvania Dutch to the northwest of Philadelphia.

It is not hard to see why so many newcomers to the American colonies chose to settle in Philadelphia or to buy land west of the Delaware under the Penn proprietorship. The site for the city of Philadelphia was very carefully chosen with regard to high ground with good drainage, a healthy location free of pests and swamps, and adequate frontage on the river that would be best for shipping, fishing, and commerce in general. Unquestionably, William Penn had the Great Fire of London of 1666 in mind when he directed his agents to make sure, in first laying out this new city in the wilderness, that "there may be ground on each side [of the houses] for gardens or orchards, or fields, that it may be a green country town, which will never be burnt, and always be wholesome."

There were several outstanding advantages to this new colony that helped it to grow more rapidly than any other settlement, in spite of its late start. First of all, religious freedom under the Quakers was a strong inducement for many different European groups. Moreover, investors in Penn's project, who bought sections of the adjoining countryside for farms, were also assigned building sites in the new town—the important thing was to make improvements in the property as soon as possible so that the land value would constantly increase for everyone. Compared to the haphazard, almost medieval growth patterns of the older parts of Boston or Manhattan—cities which it soon surpassed in size—Philadelphia began as a regular grid plan that promised orderly expansion in the future. Imposing brick town houses with fireproof slate roofs began to line the streets in imitation of the rebuilt parts of London, but the special beauty of Pennsylvania for some lay in the fact that they could create their own ethnic or religious communities away from any potential interference, since the proprietors were willing to permit a wide variety of township patterns anywhere on unclaimed lands.

The following quotation will give some idea of what the town of Philadelphia was like in 1708, as described by John Oldmixon:

> [Pennsylvania] is not the least considerable of our [British] American colonies and for the few years that the Tract of Land . . . has been inhabited, we believe none has thriv'd more, nor is more rich and populous. . . .

PHILADELPHIA, the Capital of this Colony, [is] dignify'd with the Name of a City. 'Tis indeed most commodiously situated between two navigable Rivers, the Delaware and Schoolkill [sic]. It has two Fronts on the Water . . . each Front of the City, as it was laid out, was a Mile long, and two from River to River. . . . The Houses are very stately; the Wharfs and Warehouses numerous and convenient. And as Philadelphia flourish'd so much at first, that there were near 100 Houses and cottages within less than a Year's time, so since the Foundation of this City in A.D. 1682, it has made answerable Progress; the number of Houses being computed to be 1200 now. They are generally well built, and have Orchards and Gardens. The land on which it stands is high and firm, and the Conveniency of Coves, Docks, and Springs, has very much contributed to the Commerce of this Place, where many rich Merchants now live.

The *High Street* [Market] is 100 Foot broad; so is the *Broad-street* which is in the Middle of the City, running from North to South. In the Center is a Square of 10 Acres, [planned] for the State-house, Market-house, School-house, and chief Meeting-house for the Quakers: The Land Proprietory being of that Profession [religion]; 'tis not strange that most of the first *English* Inhabitants were of same Opinion [persuasion]. The persecution rais'd by the *Popish* faction and their Adherents in England, against Protestant Dissenters, was very hot when Mr. Pen[n] obtained a *Grant* of this Territory [from Charles II], and the Quakers flock'd to it as an Asylum, from the Rage of their Enemies. But since the Glorious Revolution [1688–1689] People have transported themselves to the plantations to enrich, and not to save themselves from Injustice and Violence at home.

Men of all Principles have settled in this Place, as well as others; and there are so many orthodox professors [Anglican worshipers] that there's a great Church in Philadelphia [for them, and some] have clamoured lately for an Organ, to the great offense of the [Quaker] Brethren.

The Quakers, of course, condemned the use of music in religious services as a popish extravagance that could only divert the mind from the true contemplation of God. But then again, the basic principles of the Religious Society of Friends—universal love and toleration—could not be selectively applied to their neighbors in Pennsylvania, repeating some of the injustices they themselves had suffered before finding a safe haven. On a personal level, though, if the Quaker brethren of Philadelphia were somewhat offended by the orthodox Anglican clamor for a church organ in 1708, one wonders what they may have thought to themselves when the Anglicans decided to enlarge and completely rebuild their place of worship, Christ Church, on a sumptuous scale, beginning in 1727 and finally completing it in 1744.

Officially, Quaker taste encouraged a kind of radical simplicity in all things—from dress and speech to worldly goods and possessions—but privately, as the prosperity and population of the province soared and Philadelphia became a crowded, lively, artistic center for all of the American colonies, some of the wealthier Quaker merchants developed an appreciative eye for the finer pieces of silver and furniture being produced in their city. At the same time, the Friends' meetinghouses stanchly maintained their apparently conservative plainness when compared to buildings like Christ Church. It was a matter of low-profile Quaker meetings that were almost indistinguishable from domestic structures and Anglican ostentation, embodied most dramatically in the 196-foot steeple, the tallest in the British colonies, added to Christ Church in 1751–1754.

To find the architectural model on which Christ Church, in the second largest city of the British Empire, was based, it is not necessary to search among the series of London parish churches, each with a distinctive steeple, that Sir Christopher Wren designed after the Great Fire of 1666. Rather, it was the latest trend-setting precedent, St. Martin's-in-the Fields, London, by James Gibbs (1722–1726), that was being enthusiastically and freely adapted in Philadelphia and other towns only a short time after its completion. It appears, though, that not quite all of the expressive, classicizing, and Palladian details of the original church could be confidently reproduced by colonial craftsmen. The wooden urns adorning the decorative balustrade at the edge of the roof, for example, had to be ordered directly from London in 1735; without them the exterior would not have seemed as stylishly correct, on a par with the current fashion in the English capital—and keeping up with the latest artistic and architectural ideas was obviously on the minds of the builders and the wealthy congregation of Christ Church who were responsible for the construction.

To travel in the 1750s or 1760s from Philadelphia to any one of the German communities established upcountry was to change cultures and centuries abruptly. Such a journey would take one from eighteenth-century urban elegance (despite the crowding along narrow alleys that were not part of the original city plan for Philadelphia), past earlier settlements like Germantown, and past the splendid new country seats like Stenton and Mount Pleasant that were beginning to dot the English-owned countryside, back to a rural, medieval heritage carried over from Moravia or the Palatinate. Lumped together under a mistaken title, Pennsylvania Dutch, were German people of a variety of Protestant sects (Mennonites, Moravians, Dunkards or Brethren, Pietists, Schwenkfelders, Amish, and so forth), who began to pour into Pennsylvania after 1710, bringing their native and markedly unpretentious styles to new homes in North America.

The names of their major towns, Bethlehem and Nazareth, reflect the fact that the Moravians, members of the Renewed Church of the Brethren, were deeply inspired by evangelical ideals that made them active missionaries among the white population and among the Indians of the New World. The Pietist (Seventh Day Baptist) settlement at Ephrata was called "The Cloisters," reinforcing the sense of a semimonastic order in which the members, after taking vows of chastity and poverty, worked for the spiritual good and economic survival of the entire experimental community.

At much the same time that the huge, barnlike structures at the Ephrata Cloisters were being built according to older German precedents, the finishing touches were being added to the State House, now called Independence Hall, in Philadelphia. In these two buildings we can see the polarities of eighteenth-century thought. While individual cells at Ephrata were inhabited by celibate believers, who took the simplicity of the scriptures as a rule of faith and a model for conduct, the Supreme Court and the Assembly chambers of the State House were filled with more sophisticated men whose belief in the rule of law and the power of men's minds to follow the course of reason required a different setting.

Since the State House played such an important role as the site of the historic Second Continental Congress (1775–1776), which transformed the building into a national shrine to the concept of liberty, it is well worth revisiting the site by means of a written description published in *The Universal Magazine and Literary Museum* for 1774 (and reprinted in 1900). A high degree of civic pride shines through the writer's words as he mentions every evidence of taste or style in the architectural decoration. The shortcomings of this building on Chestnut Street, especially its modest colonial scale, compared to the huge government buildings in London, were overlooked; but journalistic accuracy required the writer to mention that the steeple was beginning to disintegrate. What follows, therefore, is a brief word-picture of the Pennsylvania State House on the eve of the Revolution, with its Georgian symmetry, its human scale, and its humanistic contents tied to English traditions still intact:

It stands about twenty five to thirty feet from the street. It is a large handsome building, two stories high, extending in front one hundred feet. On each side is a wing which joins the main building by means of a brick arcade—each of these wings is fifty feet in length. In the West wing was formerly deposited a valuable collection of books belonging to the Library Company of Philadelphia, but it is now removed to the Carpenter's Hall. . . . In the East wing are deposited the Rolls of the Province, and in the second story, the Indians [visiting delegations] make their abode when in town. These wings are arched with brick, [so] that there can be no damage in case of fire.

The State House is adorned on ye outside with rustic corners [quoins] and marble pannels, between the two storys. At your entering, you rise a flight of five steps into the entry. To the West is a large room in which the Supreme Court is held, and another on the East, in which the Assembly meet. The first of these rooms is ornamented with a breast-work and a cornish [cornice] supported by fluted pilasters of the Doric order. . . . The Assembly room is finished in a neat but not an elegant manner. From this room you go through a back door into the Assembly's library, which is a very elegant apartment. It is ornamented with a stucco ceiling and chimney places. Round the room are glass cases, in which the books are deposited. These books consist of all the laws of England made in these later years, and besides these history and poetry. . . .

In the hall is an elegant staircase which leads up to the second story, and at the head of these stairs is another hall or entry. In the room towards the East, the small arms of the city are deposited, which consist of between one and two thousand pieces, all placed in a regular manner. The room towards the West is called the Council Chamber, because it is appropriated to the Governor and Council. You then proceed into what is called the Long Room [later used by Charles Willson Peale for his portrait gallery and natural history museum]. . . .

On the top of the building is a platform surrounded on the East and West by a balustrade and on the North and South by a pallisade. From the fourth story of the steeple is a door and a handsome flight of stairs which lead up to a platform. Opposite these steps is a leaden canopy, under this the bell, on which the clock strikes. . . . The striking of the clock can be heard at any part of the city. The other part of the steeple being entirely of wood is in such a ruinous condition that they are afraid to ring the bell, lest by so doing the steeple should fall down.

In July 1776 no one was afraid to ring this bell to proclaim the fact that Independence had finally been decided upon by the delegates in convention below.

The door knocker on the Pieter Bronck House, c. 1663, West Coxsackie, New York.

RIGHT: The Demarest House, Teaneck, built
within twenty years after the first permanent
settlement in New Jersey, probably between
1678 and 1680. David Demarest, a French Protestant, emigrated with his wife and four children
to New Netherlands in 1663 and moved to New
Jersey in 1667. Irregular stonework and the
steep pitch of the roof are characteristic of the
period. The curving roof overhang was developed in the mid-seventeenth century.

ABOVE: The lower log house in Darby, Pennsylvania, dates from the 1640s. Built in a Swedish
style, with two rooms of unequal size and chimneys at each end of the house, it is thought to
be the oldest log house in the country.

Dutch House, New Castle, Delaware, c. 1665.

ABOVE: The Sinnickson chest, brought to the Delaware Valley by members of a Swedish family who settled in the colonies in the middle of the seventeenth century. Made with wrought iron bands, hinged hasps for padlocks, and two large handles, it is also painted with flower designs.

BELOW: Made in Sweden c. 1680, this chest probably belonged to an officer. It is now in the American Swedish Foundation.

ABOVE: The design of this woman's wedding chest, made in Sweden about 1650, is of Viking origin. The chest is in the American Swedish Foundation in Philadelphia.

Sleepy Hollow Church at Tarrytown, New York, was built by Frederick and Catherine Philipse of Philipsburg Manor in 1699. The roof is a typical Flemish gambrel, shaped like a flared bell with curving sides. The open octagonal belfry contains a bell cast in Holland in 1685.

Hier Leyt Begraven Het
Lichaam Van Politie Buys
Huysvrouw Van Hendrik
Van Teſsel Overleeden Den
19 Maart 1771 Out Zynde
Ontrent 65 Iaaren

Hier Lyt Het Lighaam Van
Ab:m Martlenghs Geboren Den
5:de Sep:r 1693 Ende is Overleeden
Den 22:ste April 1761 Out Zynde
67 Iaren 7 Maenden En 17 Dagen

The Abraham Hasbrouck House (c. 1692–1712), New Paltz, New York, is a fine example of the early Dutch Colonial style.

LEFT: Dutch bedroom in the 1692 part of the Hasbrouck House.

OPPOSITE: This room in the Hasbrouck House was used as the general living room at the time the house was begun in 1692. The cradle, c. 1700, is the original family one, and the Hudson Valley rush chair was made c. 1715.

OVERLEAF: Philipsburg Manor is a restoration of a seventeenth-to-early-eighteenth-century Dutch-American house and mill. In the early 1700s this was a thriving trading center.

OPPOSITE: Van Cortlandt Manor began as a rustic one-story structure used by hunters and fur traders. Pierre Van Cortlandt and his wife Joanna, upon inheriting the estate in 1748, enlarged it to its present proportions.

Entrance door to Marlpit Hall in Middletown, New Jersey. This part of the house was built in the early 1700s. Very large for its period, the divided door is noted for its beautiful paneling and bull's-eye lights.

A 17th-century Dutch *kas* from the Pieter Bronck House in West Coxsackie, New York.

OPPOSITE: Late seventeenth-century Dutch *kas* from Marlpit
Hall decorated with grisaille. The fruits, birds, and bowers
are typical motifs.

Old Swedes' Church (1698–1700), Philadelphia, Pennsylvania.

OPPOSITE: Christ Church, Philadelphia (1727), where George Washington, John Adams, Benjamin Franklin, Robert Morris, General Lafayette, and other famous patriots worshiped.

Erected in 1719, the William Trent House in Trenton is perhaps the finest traditional house in western New Jersey.

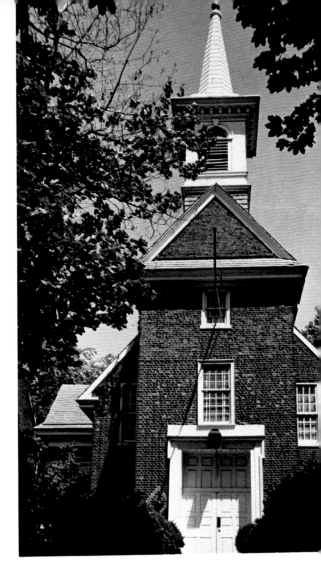

A cell in Ephrata Cloister.

OPPOSITE: The Sisters' House (1742–1743) at Ephrata Cloister, Ephrata, Pennsylvania, seen from the chapel. Of all Pennsylvania Dutch architecture, this is the most German and medieval in spirit. The monastic community combined mysticism with handicrafts and social and economic enterprises, and it boasted one of the earliest printing presses in America.

OVERLEAF: The Cloth House, c. 1750, at Ephrata Cloister.

The Martyr's Mirror Book, printed by the Ephrata Brotherhood Press, 1748–1749, the largest book printed in colonial America. Translated from the Dutch into German at the request of the Mennonites, it was widely circulated in Southeastern Pennsylvania.

The Wilson–Warner House, 1769, Odessa, Delaware. The present house was constructed as an addition to an earlier one built c. 1740, which was owned by David Wilson, a prosperous merchant.

Stenton, Germantown, Pennsylvania, built in 1728. Its completely regular façade is an example of the early Georgian style in America.

OPPOSITE: A view of the staircase at Stenton as seen from the entrance hall.

A detail of the mouse-tooth brick triangles that ornament the gable and the Dutch cross-bond brickwork on the Leendert Bronck House, c. 1738, in West Coxsackie, New York.

The Dey Mansion, c. 1740–1750, in Passaic County, New Jersey, is a classical expression of New Netherlands architectural traditions.

This eighteenth-century *kas,* made in Bergen County, comes from the Dey Mansion.

OPPOSITE: The door knocker from the Dey Mansion.

OVERLEAF: Wig stand in a bedroom at Van Cortlandt Manor in New York.

The Old State House (Independence Hall) in Philadelphia, built 1731–1736 in the Georgian style. The tower was erected in 1750; the wooden steeple was not completed until 1753. Tower and steeple, removed in 1781, were rebuilt in 1828 along their original lines.

St. Paul's Chruch, Eastchester, New York, built in 1768, reflects the Renaissance revival in the colonies.

OPPOSITE: The Supreme Court chamber in Independence Hall. Here English law was administered until the Revolution, and here, on July 8, 1776, the King's coat of arms was torn down and burned in defiance of royal authority.

This downstairs room in the Vorleezer House, Richmond Town, Staten Island, New York, contains furniture from the early to mid-eighteenth century.

Moravian plank chair, dating from the 1750s, is still in the Whitfield House, where it was originally used.

Hinge originally used in the Christian Springs Moravian Settlement (founded 1747), now in the Whitfield House, Nazareth, Pennsylvania.

Mid-eighteenth-century table in typical German style from the Milbach bedroom in the Philadelphia Museum of Art.

This serpentine was used in an orchestra in Bethlehem, Pennsylvania, as early as 1753. A bass instrument of wood, covered with leather and pierced with finger holes, its ancestors were in use in ancient Egypt. The serpentine as seen here was developed in the sixteenth century and was popular in church music until the early seventeenth century.

OVERLEAF: Valley Forge, Pennsylvania, where Washington's troops camped, is today a State park.

131

Old Tennant Church in Freehold, New Jersey, dates back to 1751. It was built by a congregation of Scottish Presbyterians who received a charter from George II in 1749.

The Bell House, 1745–1746, in Bethlehem, Pennsylvania, reveals a distinct German influence in its architecture.

OPPOSITE: The Dickenson House, near Alloway, New Jersey, was built in 1754. The use of ornate glazed brickwork in flat zigzag patterns derives from medieval folk sources.

Old Drawyer's Church (1773), near Odessa. This simple structure was built in the Quaker style by a Scottish-Irish congregation. A deviation from the ultimate simplicity of Quaker meetinghouses is seen in the columned and pedimented entrance.

ABOVE: Expertly crafted exterior beehive decoration of the Corbit–Sharp House, Odessa, Delaware.

The Corbit–Sharp House was built 1772–1774 by William Corbit near the banks of Appoquinimink Creek, above the site of his tannery. The house is maintained by the Henry Francis du Pont Winterthur Museum.

The Cecil Bedroom in the Winterthur Museum, from an early eighteenth-century Maryland house, has a unique pad-foot maple bed from Rhode Island with eighteenth-century crewel embroidery hangings.

OPPOSITE: Mount Pleasant, Fairmount Park, Philadelphia, built 1761–1762 by John Macpherson, a Scottish sea captain and privateer who furnished his home in the height of Chippendale fashion.

RIGHT: American Chippendale chair, possibly made by Benjamin Randolph, a leading furniture maker of Philadelphia, sometime between 1760 and 1775, and now in the Henry Francis du Pont collection at Winterthur, Delaware.

BELOW: Detail of the distinctive hairy paw foot of the chair at right.

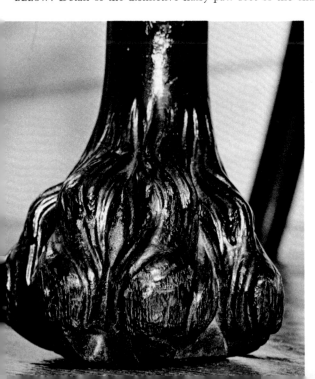

III

TIDEWATER TOWNS
AND
SOUTHERN PLANTATIONS

In the Southern colonies along the Atlantic coast—that is to say, from the shores of Chesapeake Bay and its tributaries southward to the mouth of the Savannah River—geography and climate combined to produce fundamental differences in settlement and agricultural patterns. The English colonists early in the seventeenth century were delighted to find that major crops, such as corn, tobacco, and later rice in the Carolinas, did very well in Southern soil, but the villages they planted, beginning with the crude shelters inside the triangular fort at Jamestown in 1607, never grew with the same vigor evident in the North. Only Williamsburg, Annapolis, and Charleston, South Carolina, seem to be exceptions to the rule that population in the South remained widely dispersed, anti-urban, and therefore limited in size. This regional disparity in total numbers became especially significant during the Civil War when the South had to draw its armies from only about five and a half million whites, while the Northern states had a population of close to twenty million.

The initial difficulties encountered by the English in their attempts to colonize Virginia are well known. The idea was to gain a foothold on the North American continent somewhere in the cartographic void between Spanish claims to the entire Caribbean, including Florida, to the south and French control of Canada (La Nouvelle France) to the north. As early as 1585, under a patent from Queen Elizabeth, Sir Walter Raleigh sent out an expedition to Roanoke Island (now North Carolina). However, the colony that existed there in 1587 had completely disappeared when a resupply mission was able to return in 1590. The site was abandoned.

At the beginning of its history seventeen years later, the London Company outpost at Jamestown was almost as tragically unsuccessful. Half of the colonists died during the late summer and fall of 1607. Dissension was rife, verging on mutiny among the men, many of them well-

141

Elfreth's Alley in Philadelphia, a street that has seen little change since colonial times.

born, who came to get rich quick on silver and gold, not to put in long hours of hard work each day for the communal good rather than their own profit. And the winter of 1609–1610 was called the "starving time" by the sixty or so dispirited souls who survived out of a community of five hundred.

The history of this early settlement in Virginia has been described as a woeful tale of "famine, disease, misfortune, and disappointments." There was famine because the colonists did not store their food carefully enough to prevent spoilage and pests. Disease came as the result of malnutrition, an alien climate, and exposure—adequate frame or brick houses were not built until much later, reflecting a lack of effective discipline. The single greatest misfortune the colony suffered was in arousing the implacable hostility of the neighboring tribes under Powhatan. Skirmishes took place on and off during the early years, many of them led by Captain John Smith, who was himself caught and almost put to death. Later, in spite of the marriage between John Rolfe and Pocahontas that was supposed to insure peaceful coexistence, an all-out Indian attack in 1624 killed fully a third of the white population. From the point of view of shareholders in the London Company, moreover, the biggest disappointments in their New World venture came with the failure to find precious metals immediately, followed by the unprofitable attempts to start local industries and the impossibility of building a miniature thriving London on an unhealthy site, surrounded by marshes.

The true wealth of the tidewater colonies, Virginia and neighboring Maryland, lay in farming the land, not in ill-advised mining or manufacturing projects. Scholars have shown that as early as 1619 the two essential factors for the future economy of the South were present in this area. First, a single crop, tobacco, had already become the leading export of this English colony only seven years after its introduction by the planter John Rolfe. Cotton, of course, would not be "king" until the nineteenth century when the invention of the cotton gin (1793) and the weaving mills spawned by the Industrial Revolution vastly increased the demand for this cheap fiber—until that time tobacco was the basis for countless fortunes as long as cheap labor was available. Significantly, 1619 was also the year in which the first African slaves arrived in Virginia aboard a Dutch ship. After that, profit margins soared as the wealthy planters discovered the advantages of using unpaid slaves, instead of indentured white servants, to plant, cultivate, and harvest hundreds of acres of tobacco in the hot sun. As one English commentator put it, "Tobacco is the standing Commodity of the Country, and [it] is so beneficial to the Planter, and so natural to the soil, that all other Improvements give place to that. Indeed, they could turn their Hands to nothing that would employ so many Slaves and Servants, and require so little Stock to manage it, or take up such a large Tract of Land."

Among English consumers, "Virginia Leaf" was in demand for its mild, flavorful qualities when smoked, but it could also be aged, fermented, and pulverized to be taken as snuff. Brand names came into existence, such as "Best Virginia" and "Best York River," to signify the New World origin of the product, and specialty shops opened dealing just in tobacco in its various salable forms—wound in a roll, shredded to be smoked in pipes, made into snuff, or ready to

142

chew. According to several writers on folk art traditions, a popular misconception arose in the English mind early in the seventeenth century. The idea of the American Indian who grew and used tobacco long before the arrival of the white man was somehow confused with the Virginia planter who raised the weed as a cash crop and with the black slaves who actually tended the tobacco fields on Virginia plantations. As the result of this confusion, wooden figures called "Black Boys" or "Virginians," wearing headdresses and kilts of tobacco leaves, carrying a roll or rope of tobacco under one arm and offering to share a long-stemmed pipe with the other, became standard store-front emblems for London tobacconists. Needless to say, these early shop figures were the ancestors of whole tribes of cigar-store Indians in America in the nineteenth century.

In his monumental survey, *The Making of Urban America; A History of City Planning in the United States,* John W. Reps has demonstrated the vital importance of agriculture and topography in defining how land was actually used in colonial Maryland and Virginia. In certain respects the waterways were just as important as the land surface itself. In terms of transportation, for example, Chesapeake Bay offered unique advantages. Since the rivers flowing into it (especially the Potomac, the Rappahannock, the York, and the James) were navigable so far inland from the coast, there was no need for a single city (like Boston) to serve as a principal port of entry for the entire tidewater area. The export of raw materials and the return of English manufactured goods was made infinitely easier by the fact that both sides of the bay and both banks of the major tributaries were directly accessible to ocean-going ships.

Southern settlement patterns were also affected by the early discovery that a cash crop, such as tobacco, became increasingly profitable in direct proportion to the number of acres under cultivation. For this reason the wealthier planters began to amass huge estates through government grants (for bringing more settlers or servants into the colony) or through outright purchase. Vast tracts were necessary for a maximum profit because of the traditional but rather wasteful method of farming the land. Once the forest had been cleared and the stumps removed, a particular field could be planted with the same crop for only a few years in succession, perhaps five at the most, before the soil became exhausted. Without fertilizers to restore the depleted chemicals, these overworked fields were simply left fallow for a decade or two while the soil renewed itself.

Even as early as the 1630s the differences between Massachusetts Bay and Chesapeake Bay must have been obvious to anyone who visited both regions. Where a New England village (surrounded by relatively small, privately owned fields) was a social and political unit, preserving and protecting the equal rights of its residents, a colonial plantation in the South was basically an economic division of the land under the controlling authority of a single owner. This centralized authority was clearly expressed in the nature and position of the main house as a symbol of family power and prestige. In order to supervise the day-to-day activities on their plantations and to have direct communication with the outside world, virtually all tidewater landowners preferred "to have their houses near the water for the convenience of trade, and their lands on each side and behind their homes."

To personalize these regional differences it is tempting to compare the lives of contemporaries, such as Adam Thoroughgood in Virginia and Thomas Hooker in Massachusetts. Hooker, a Puritan clergyman, was a dedicated nonconformist; in 1636 he led a group of dissidents westward through the New England wilderness to the Connecticut River, where they helped to found the town of Hartford according to standard village patterns. In this rude but tightly knit frontier community one may assume that no man's house, not even the Reverend Hooker's, was allowed to overreach its neighbors in size or decoration.

By contrast, Adam Thoroughgood was undoubtedly an Anglican and well-born, although temporarily strapped for funds in 1621 when he came to the New World as an identured servant. In a very short time, however, he paid off his passage price, established himself as a free man, and even won election as a burgess to the Virginia Assembly (1629). By 1636 he had received title to a patent of 5350 acres in Princess Anne County, bordering on Lynnhaven Bay, and there he began to build a brick house (possibly the oldest surviving dwelling in the English colonies) that was left to his wife, Sarah, when he died in 1640. Despite its status as a key monument in the early history of American domestic architecture, the Adam Thoroughgood House is quite small—only two rooms on the first floor, a hall and a parlor—in keeping with seventeenth-century examples in other areas. But for its time and place, it must have been impressive, particularly because of the brickwork—a permanent material compared to the timber frame structures, erected by the first Virginia settlers, which quickly decayed in the humid climate.

As a specific type, the Thoroughgood House can be described as a direct ancestor of the rural farmhouses in Virginia that were built during the second half of the seventeenth century. As a planter's home, however, logically built in the midst of extensive properties, it also predicted future arrangements of this kind on a grander scale. Our modern mental picture of a Southern plantation in colonial times is based on eighteenth-century examples, such as Mulberry Plantation, Berkeley County, South Carolina (c. 1714), Stratford, Westmoreland County (1725–1730), Westover, Charles City County (1730–1734), Carter's Grove, James City County (1750–1753), and Shirley, Charles City County (1769), Virginia. These Georgian classics have established the standard image of a prosperous plantation house as a beautiful brick mansion, stately and proud, presenting one majestic façade to the water's edge and the other to the fertile lands behind.

Guests were always welcome in these mansions, whether they arrived by boat or by horse and carriage. Southern hospitality was legendary, even in the early 1700s. According to Oldmixon's survey of *The British Empire in America,* the tidewater colonists were an especially "prudent, careful, generous, hospitable People; their Houses being open to all Travellers, whom they entertain as heartily as Relations or Friends. . . . As for the Convenience of Society, the Gentlemens' Houses are at not much greater distance from one another than they are in *England.* The Planters are almost all sociable; and as everything towards making their Friends welcome is cheaper than in *England,* so the Entertainments there are larger, the Reception more sincere, and the Mirth of the Company more hearty than in most of our Gentlemens' Houses."

In strictly formal terms, these Southern plantation houses tended to be large rectangular blocks, containing the standard four-room-and-entryway plan on the ground floor—with the inviting entrances tastefully emphasized in the center of each façade. Compared to their northern cousins, these eighteenth-century mansions seem even larger, more graceful, and more conscious of what was currently in fashion in London. Symmetrically placed dependencies, for example, sometimes attached to the main house (following English interpretations of Palladio) were a prominent feature in the South. And this closer connection with the parent country is not surprising since the wharf built out into the tidewater by each plantation owner was a direct link—no middlemen involved—with life in the English capital. Goods as well as services could be purchased in England and shipped back to one's doorstep without delay.

As a further note, the popularity and importance of Palladian designs—from projecting temple-front porticoes to a particular type of three-part window with an arch over the taller central section—should be mentioned since they appear so frequently in colonial architecture of the third quarter of the eighteenth century. For his original clients in the Veneto of the mid-1500s, the Italian Renaissance architect Palladio created exquisitely beautiful and entirely functional rural villas which James S. Ackerman has perceptively described as the best of both worlds, "the farmer's and the gentleman's." Transmitted through design books, Palladian principles of strict order and symmetry in plan and elevation were adopted by English architects and theorists of the early Georgian era as an antidote to the excesses of the Wren-Baroque style.

In the American Colonies a generation later, one might expect to see a wholehearted adoption of the severe Palladian style, but this did not happen. The Miles Brewton House in Charleston (1765–1769) is one of the few examples that can be pointed to as being drawn directly from one of the plates in Palladio's own *Four Books of Architecture,* but this building was a town house, not a rural villa. In his authoritative discussion of Palladian influence on colonial architecture, William H. Pierson, Jr., has pointed out that its impact was noticeably stronger in the South at this time than elsewhere, no doubt because the needs of plantation owners for buildings that would express their station in the world, while keeping them close to their fields and crops, matched the demands originally made on Palladio by his patrons. However, Pierson demonstrates that this influence was rarely unmixed in America. At Mount Airy in Richmond County, Virginia (1758–1762), for instance, one finds that the ground plan of the villa and its attached dependencies is completely Palladian in spirit, but the decorative surfaces of the house—the rusticated joints in the brown sandstone masonry versus the lighter trim and detailing—was derived from plates in English design books, particularly from plates by James Gibbs, who perpetuated the older taste. From Palladio came the insistence on axial order and symmetry that made Southern plantation houses seem more monumental, controlled, and aristocratic than ever before.

In the absence of urban settlements most plantation houses also had to serve as oases of culture in addition to entertainment. While the large, high-ceilinged, and elegantly appointed room, often called the "Great Hall," was the center for social gatherings and dances, a library was also an indispensable attribute for any educated gentleman. It is easy to imagine the pleasure involved in the arrival of the latest ship, bringing an awaited order from a London bookseller. At Westover, William Byrd II, one of the richest men in Virginia, accumulated a library of more than 3600 volumes, and his surviving diaries, which have been reprinted in the twentieth century, afford an intimate glimpse of how much he enjoyed quiet intellectual pursuits in private as opposed to his public role as a landowner and member of the Assembly.

To gain some sense of what the largest plantations were like in full operation one has to imagine dozens of outbuildings, including slave quarters, making up a self-sufficient village under the watchful eyes of the proprietor or his foremen. While the master's family lived and entertained in the main house, most of the domestic woman's work of the plantation—the "drudgeries of cookery, washing, dairies, etc."—were performed in the nearby "offices," kept apart from the mansion so that it might remain "cool and sweet."

Still farther from the main building one would expect to find a number of sheds where semi-skilled male slaves turned the natural products of the plantation into usable goods for home use. Animal skins could be tanned in one shed and turned into shoes for other slaves in another. Wool or vegetable fibers could be spun into yarn and then woven into rough cloth for garments or blankets. Trees cut down as more fields were cleared provided logs to burn as well as lumber for construction purposes from major posts and beams to shingles and clapboards. It was relatively easy work to erect barns or slave quarters, but more talented black carpenters were also used to do interior paneling—sometimes under the supervision of English master carpenters and joiners imported just for the purpose of finishing a magnificent home in the richest possible manner.

Closer to the barns and stables, the blacksmith was kept extremely busy at his forge, shoeing a great many horses, fixing broken implements, and making basic items of hardware such as hinges and nails. Nearby another slave was probably employed full-time as a cooper, making numerous wooden vessels, from washtubs to the casks in which the dried tobacco was stored in the plantation's warehouse, waiting to be shipped abroad. In still another shed the seasonal fruits of the orchard might be transformed into jugs of cider or distilled in brandies of various flavors. And all of this was made possible, of course, by the cheapness of the labor in the fields, the gangs of black slaves, living well out of sight of the main house, who did the annual digging, sowing, weeding, harvesting, gleaning, and turning the earth over again for each new crop year after year until they were too sick or too old to work—or tried to run away.

The completely independent lives of rich plantation owners did not take well, it seems, to citification. In tidewater Maryland and Virginia, having a single major city through which all goods would pass might have been more convenient for colonial administrators who were empowered to collect a tax on incoming and outgoing cargoes, but there was no advantage in this for the large or the small farmers. As colonial capitals, Jamestown in Virginia and St. Mary's in Maryland never prospered in the seventeenth century, and in both cases the seat of government in the province was moved to a new site in the 1690s.

Jamestown had never been a particularly happy choice, and rebels under Nathaniel Bacon had set fire to the place in 1676. When the capital of Virginia was transferred from the rebuilt but still far from prospering Jamestown to Middle Plantation in 1699, this far healthier site, renamed Williamsburg, consisted only of a church, an ordinary (meaning a public house), several stores, two mills, a smithy, a grammar school, and, above all, William and Mary College—with its main building attributed to Sir Christopher Wren then under construction.

In planning this new capital, the Assembly, under Governor Francis Nicholson, drew up very specific laws to control the distribution of the land, the style and placement of the "two fine Publick Buildings in this Country" (the College and the Capitol or State-House), and size and setbacks of the private dwellings, including the Governor's Palace. Far behind Boston, Newport, New Haven, New York, and Philadelphia in terms of population to start with, Williamsburg was planned for only about two thousand inhabitants—with accommodations, of course, "suitable for the reception of a considerable number and concourse of people, that of necessity must resort to the place where the general assemblies will be convened, and where the council and supreme court of justice for his majesty's colony and dominion will be held and kept."

As described by Hugh Jones in *The Present State of Virginia* (London, 1724), Williamsburg was a very domestic town in the eighteenth century. A peaceful and logical order was evident everywhere, thanks to the regular plan and the fact that the houses, fronting alike on a common six-foot setback from the street, were rather widely spaced to prevent the spread of fire that threatened all colonial settlements. The ideal of domestic architecture in this community —an ideal that is beautifully embodied in the Wythe House, which fronts on the Palace Green— was a fine brick house that would always be "lasting dry, and warm in winter, and cool in summer." Given the nature of the climate, the spacing between dwellings, like the central passageway through the center of each one (together with the larger sash windows of the eighteenth century), had an additional benefit; these openings provided "a free passage for the air, which is very grateful in violent hot weather"—then as now.

Until the time of the Revolution Williamsburg remained a place where men could "dwell comfortably, genteely, pleasantly, and plentifully" in the heart of the Old Dominion, but political change and the westward, inland expansion of the state demanded the relocation of the capital. After 1779, when the new Commonwealth of Virginia moved its legislative functions to Richmond, Williamsburg began to decline. In the early nineteenth century travelers noted that it "is now little better than a *deserted village*," calling forth the inevitable train of melancholy associations. Well-subsidized restorations in the 1930s rescued the town from oblivion, making it a national attraction, but we should never overlook the fact that the Early Georgian style of architecture in the public buildings at Williamsburg was thoroughly rejected as ugly and old-fashioned by men such as Thomas Jefferson who sought a new era in political freedom as well as new symbolic ideas in architectural forms.

The early years of the new capital of Maryland were less traumatic, perhaps, than the rise and fall of Williamsburg, but the history of Annapolis also tends to show how difficult it was to plan and build a tidewater town that would quickly reach and then maintain at least a minimum density. The town was laid out in 1695, using an unusual combination of public circles and residential squares based on European planning concepts that were not completely understood. However, when the moving force behind the project, Francis Nicholson, was made governor of Virginia three years later, momentum was lost. The following oft-quoted report of 1708 offers some indication of what the settlement on the banks of the Severn looked like in the first decade of the eighteenth century:

> Governor Nicholson had done his Endeavour to make a Town of that Place. There are about 40 Dwelling Houses in it, 7 or 8 of which can afford a good lodging and Accommodations for strangers. There are also a State-House [burned 1704 and rebuilt], and a free school, built with brick, which make a great show among a Parcel of wooden Houses; and the foundation of a Church is laid, the only Brick Church in Maryland. They have two Market days in a Week; and had Governor Nicholson continu'd for a few years longer, he [would have] brought it to Perfection.

As in Charleston, South Carolina (founded 1680), and Savannah, Georgia (established 1733)—two other ports that also served as provincial capitals—prosperity and expansion in Annapolis came in the middle and later part of the 1700s. The Maryland State House in Annapolis (begun in 1772) is evidence of the increasing wealth of the colony in public terms, while private homes, some of them designed or at least decorated by William Buckland, set new standards of refinement, visual elegance, and meticulous detailing in colonial residential buildings of the 1760s and 1770s. We should be especially grateful in the case of Annapolis that all the eighteenth-century charms of a peaceful tidewater town have not been sacrificed on the altar of twentieth-century progress and land development.

Finally, in looking back at the impressive façades of Southern mansions, especially Mount Vernon and Monticello, we are reminded that the educated Virginia aristocracy were more than just provincial English gentlemen. Aesthetically, they may have followed a variety of imported tastes, but they also guided the Revolution and brought the Republic through its first decades of independence from the Crown.

In Jefferson's case, rejection of British rule brought a corollary abandonment of the traditional Georgian colonial style. He was governor of Virginia when the state capital was moved to Richmond, and his design for the new Capitol building (1785–1788) was directly based on Greco-Roman precedents. While admiring our colonial architectural heritage for its honesty, its intimate human scale, and its undisguised use of simple materials, we must also realize that men of the first generation after the Revolution, men like Thomas Jefferson, searched far back into history to find an architectural style associated with the freedom of a republic, untainted by the ecclesiastical or monarchial controls so deeply despised by Americans who had fought so long for their liberty as a nation.

148

The Jerusalem Church, Savannah, Georgia, was built 1767–1769 by the Salzburger Lutherans.

Bacon's Castle, built 1649–c. 1665 by Arthur Allen in Surry County, Virginia, the sole surviving example of full Jacobean design and the first cross-plan house in Virginia. Brick walls laid in English bond have decorative end gables with free-standing triple chimneys of medieval inspiration. Nathaniel Bacon's adherents seized the house in the rebellion of 1676.

OPPOSITE: The Adam Thoroughgood House (c. 1636–1640) near Norfolk is the oldest house in Virginia and the archetype of the colony's substantial farmhouses of the latter half of the century. The walls are English bond brickwork on three sides and Flemish bond in front.

Doll in the Mary Washington House, Fredericksburg, Virginia.

Jacobean Court Cupboard made in Virginia c. 1660 and now in the Old Salem Museum, Old Salem, North Carolina.

Rinsing bowl and wine glass which belonged to Mary Washington, mother of George Washington. Many wines were served with dinner, and the glass was rinsed between each one. Bowl and glass are in the Mary Washington House, Fredericksburg, Virginia.

OVERLEAF: The Magazine in Williamsburg was erected in 1715 to house arms and ammunition sent from England for the defense of the colony.

Lock on the front door of Bacon's Castle (page 150).

Courtroom in the Capitol.

OPPOSITE: The Capitol in Williamsburg, originally built 1701–1704, was twice burned (in 1747 and 1832), rebuilt, and finally restored in 1928–1934 according to the original plan. From 1704 to 1780 Virginia's House of Burgesses, America's oldest representative assembly, met here. Fire, candles, and smoking were forbidden in the first building; in 1723 restrictions were relaxed and two chimneys were added.

Catechism in the Mary Washington House, Fredericksburg.

Silver from the George Wythe House, Williamsburg.

OPPOSITE: Wig stand and bowl in the Williamsburg barbershop.

Dictionary in the Wren building (page 160) was printed in London in 1671.

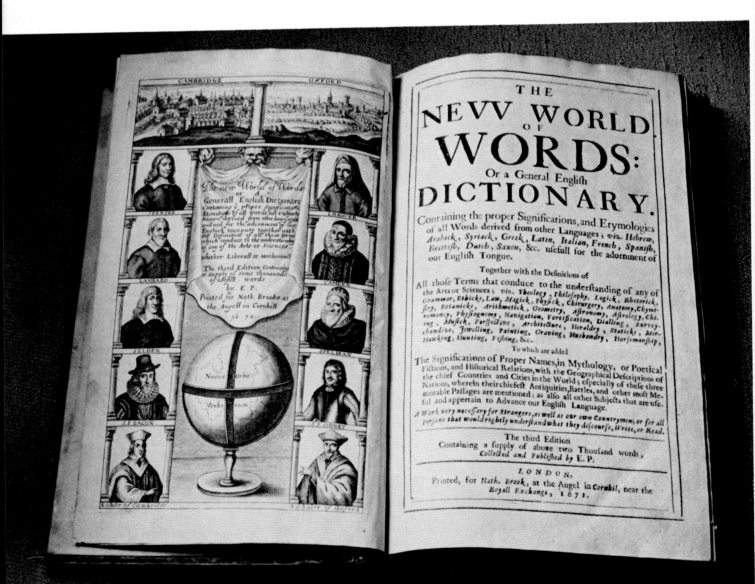

OPPOSITE: The design of the Wren building, Williamsburg, the oldest academic building in the English-speaking colonies in continuous use since its opening, is attributed to Sir Christopher Wren. The cornerstone was laid in 1695. The building today appears substantially as it was in 1716.

Reconstructed servants' quarters on the Elkanah Deane property in Williamsburg. From 1750 on, an outside stairway kept the upper and lower floors completely separate.

OPPOSITE: The King's Arms kitchen garden in Williamsburg.

OVERLEAF: A bedroom in the Peyton Randolph house in Williamsburg.

OPPOSITE: Outbuildings on the George Wythe property, seen from the main house
With the gardens, they form a plantation layout in miniature.

An upstairs bedroom in the Brush–Everard House, Williamsburg.

OVERLEAF: The Wythe House was built in 1754 by George Wythe, one of the most influential citizens of his time, a classical scholar, and the first professor of law at an American college. Thomas Jefferson was one of his students at William and Mary. Sheep graze on the Palace Green in Williamsburg as they did two hundred years ago.

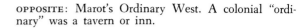

OPPOSITE: Marot's Ordinary West. A colonial "ordinary" was a tavern or inn.

The Bruton Parish Church in Williamsburg, completed in 1715. The Anglican Church and the state were united in early colonial Virginia.

The Red Lion Inn, built in the early 1700s; shown here as reconstructed. The checkerboard pattern in glazed brick became popular early in the eighteenth century.

OVERLEAF: Unrestored eighteenth-century marbleizing in Holly Hill, Friendship, Maryland. The painting, dated c. 1730, is set in the original marbled woodwork.

The slave quarters at Boone Hall Plantation outside Charleston, South Carolina. The land was granted to John Boone in 1676 by the Lord Proprietors in England. Slave labor manufactured brick tile on the 17,000-acre cotton plantation.

The central block of Mulberry Plantation, South Carolina, 1714, is laid in English bond brickwork. Four unique corner pavilions with hipped roofs and bell-shaped turrets, similar to those of seventeenth-century France, are the result of Huguenot influence.

Tuckahoe, in Goochland County, Virginia, built 1710–1730 in an H-plan with two dependencies in front of the main building.

RIGHT: Tulip Hill, Anne Arundel County, Maryland, c. 1756, was built by Samuel Galloway, a Quaker who was read out of Friends' Meeting for importing slaves. He built the house himself, working from English textbooks. The entrance portico is thought to be a later addition, and wings were added c. 1790. The house was named for the tulip trees on the property.

The Great Hall at Carter's Grove.

BELOW: The front hallway and stairway in Tulip Hill are by William Buckland.

The culmination of Virginia's early Georgian style is seen in Carter's Grove, built 1750–1753 by Carter Burwell in James City County. The balanced dependencies were once completely detached.

The west or land façade of Drayton Hall (c. 1738–1742), Charleston, South Carolina, has a projecting two-story portico and superimposed Doric and Ionic orders, a conception stemming directly from Palladio. The house was built for John Drayton, a member of the King's Council.

The Great Hall fireplace in Drayton Hall.

The garden at Gunston Hall, Lorton, Virginia.

View of Gunston Hall from the garden. The house was built between 1755 and 1758 by George Mason, author of the Virginia Declaration of Rights and member of the Federal Constitutional Convention.

The Ladies' Diary: or Woman's Almanack, printed in 1770, from the collection at Gunston Hall.

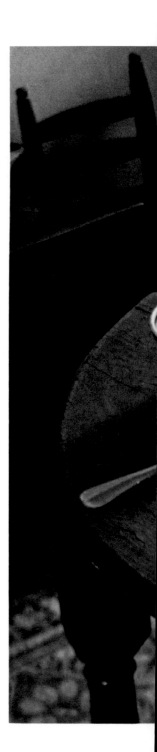

A child's walker, Gunston Hall.

A children's tea set, Gunston Hall.

Detail of a doorway in the Palladian room at Gunston Hall.

The wood carving in the Palladian room and all of the carving and joining of the interiors of Gunston Hall were done by William Buckland.

Mount Airy in Richmond County, built in 1758–62 by Colonel John Tayloe on land acquired by his grandfather in the 1650s, is one of the few Virginia houses built of stone during the eighteenth century and the first in the colonies to achieve the full Palladian villa scheme.

OVERLEAF: Wild Heron Plantation, fifteen miles from Savannah, Georgia, was built c. 1752–1756 on land granted to John Rogerson in 1747 by the Trustees of the Colony. The moss-covered oaks have survived colonial times.

The drawing room or "Great Hall" of Sotterley (c. 1725), Hollywood, Maryland, has mid-eighteenth-century paneling with matching alcoves of carved wood. The house was built by James Bowles, a wealthy Englishman, who died in 1727. His widow, Rebecca Addison Bowles, in 1729 married George Plater II, a successful lawyer, who changed Sotterley from a simple plantation house into a mansion.

The Chinese Chippendale staircase and the shell alcoves in the Sotterley drawing room were both done by an indentured servant, Richard Boulton.

View from the Great Hall into the Chinese parlor at White-hall, Anne Arundel County, Maryland (pages 192–193). The house, rich in ornamentation and classical details, was built 1764–1765 as the residence of Governor Horatio Sharpe of Maryland. It was not unusual for buildings steeped in English tradition to be built on the edge of the wilderness. In the absence of appropriate materials or craftsmen, wooden carvings were made to imitate stone or were sized to the walls in emulation of European plaster decoration.

Chowan County Courthouse, 1767, Edenton, North Carolina.

The interior of Aquia Church on Aquia Creek, Stafford County (1757), a fine example of original woodwork in a Virginia church.

The south façade of Whitehall. The opulent Corinthian columns of the portico, made of white cedar logs, rest in bases of sandstone and molded brick.

The north façade of Whitehall. The Palladian house had a garden or water entrance as well as one in front. In 1773 Governor Sharpe of Maryland, who built the house, returned to England. Upon his death in 1790 the house was willed to John Ridout, who added the second story to the central block of the house in 1793.

OVERLEAF: The great square hall or salon of Whitehall occupies the full depth of the house. It seems certain that William Buckland was responsible for the ornate carved decoration throughout the house.

193

Montpelier, Prince George County, Maryland, built c. 1750.
Wings were added c. 1770.

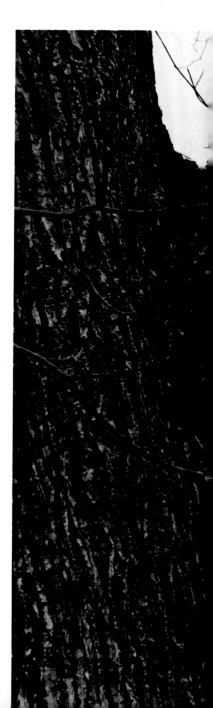

Shirley Plantation in Charles City County, Virginia, built
by Charles Carter in 1769. The influence of Palladio is seen
again here in the two classic porticoes on the north and south
sides, topped by pediments.

The Holmes Bookcase, c. 1770, attributed to Thomas Elfe, one of Charleston's most prominent furniture makers, is in the Heywood–Washington House in Charleston, South Carolina.

OPPOSITE: The Chase–Lloyd House, Annapolis, Maryland, 1769–1771, was begun in 1769 by Samuel Chase, one of the signers of the Declaration of Independence. In 1771 he sold it to Colonel Edward Lloyd IV, who hired William Buckland to create the magnificent interior of the house.

A butterfly hinge on the window shutter in the Chase–Lloyd House.

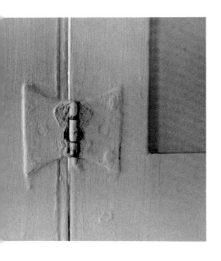

The main feature of the house is an entrance hall dominated by an oversize window and a cantilevered stairway which divides at the landing, framing and further emphasizing the great Palladian window.

Brass lock in the dining-room door.

The John Stuart House, Charleston, South Carolina. The old seaport was a summer resort of colonial America. Here the eighteenth-century Georgian houses have a distinctly Southern flavor; pastel colors covering old brick and stucco give the city a foreign look.

A detail of the window molding from the Hammond–Harwood House (1773–1774) in Annapolis, Maryland. This Georgian house was built by Matthias Hammond, a lawyer whose income was derived from his fifty-four tobacco plantations. The work is attributed to William Buckland.

Belarmine ware and jars from the Hammond–Harwood House, Annapolis.

OPPOSITE: Collection of eighteenth-century pewter in the Hammond–Harwood House. Everything is American except the large teakettle. Pewter was widely used, and pewter poisoning was not uncommon.

OVERLEAF: The Flock Room in the Winterthur Museum in New Castle County, Delaware, depicts an eighteenth-century room from a Virginia plantation house. The green and gray flock covering on the walls, made of cut-up wool applied to a pattern glued on canvas, simulates cut velvet. The chairs are from New England, but the paneling is from an old Virginia house.

Monticello. Thomas Jefferson designed and built his home near Charlottesville, Virginia, from 1770 to 1775. Although he much altered and enlarged the house between 1796 and 1809, its Palladian character was consistently maintained.

OPPOSITE: A French pier mirror in the parlor of Monticello reflects the marble and ormolu clock on the mantelpiece.

Jefferson's bedroom in Monticello.

OVERLEAF: Mount Vernon, Fairfax County, Virginia. When George Washington acquired the house in 1752, it was a story-and-a-half high, with a central hall and four small rooms on the first floor. Over the years the house was expanded; the last addition was completed in 1787.

SELECTED BIBLIOGRAPHY

Ackerman, James S. *Palladio*. Baltimore, 1966.

Anonymous. *A Short Narrative of the Horrid Massacre in Boston, perpetrated in the evening of the fifth day of March, 1770, by soldiers of the 29th regiment*. Boston, 1770. Reprinted New York, 1849.

Anonymous. *Massachusettensis; or, A Series of Letters, containing a Faithful State of Many Important and Striking Facts, which laid the Foundation of the Present Troubles in the Province of the Masachusetts-Bay*. 3rd ed. Boston, 1776.

Beirne, Rosalind Randall. *William Buckland, 1734–1774; Architect of Virginia and Maryland*. Baltimore, 1958.

Bradford, William. *History of Plymouth Plantation, 1620–1647*. 2 vols. Boston, 1912.

Bridenbaugh, Carl. *Cities in the Wilderness; The First Century of Urban Life in America, 1625–1742*. New York, 1938.

Briggs, Martin S. *Homes of the Pilgrim Fathers in England and America, 1620–1685*. London, 1932.

Buhler, Kathryn C., and Graham Hood. *American Silver: Garvan and other Collections in the Yale University Art Gallery*. 2 vols. New Haven, 1970.

Camesasca, Ettore, ed. *History of the House*. Translated by Isabel Quigly. New York, 1971.

Carson, Jane, ed. *We Were There; Descriptions of Williamsburg, 1699–1859*. Williamsburg, Va., 1965.

Cummings, Abbott Lowell. "Decorative Painting in Seventeenth-Century New England," in *American Painting to 1776; A Reappraisal: Winterthur Conference Report 1971*. Winterthur, 1971. Pp. 71–125.

———, ed. *Rural Household Inventories; Establishing the Names, Uses, and Furnishings of Rooms in the Colonial New England Home, 1675–1775*. Boston, 1964.

Davidson, Marshall B. *The American Heritage Book of Historic American Houses*. New York, 1970.

Forbes, Hariette Merrifield. *Gravestones of Early New England and the Men Who Made Them, 1653–1800*. Boston, 1927.

Forman, Henry Chandlee. *Maryland Architecture; A Short History from 1634 through the Civil War*. Cambridge, Md., 1968.

Garvan, Anthony N. B. *Architecture and Town Planning in Colonial Connecticut*. New Haven, 1951.

Gowans, Alan. *Images of American Living; Four Centuries of Architecture and Furniture as Cultural Expression*. Philadelphia and New York, 1964.

Hatch, Charles E., Jr. *Jamestown, Virginia; The Townsite and Its Story*. National Park Service Historical Handbook Series, no. 2. Rev. ed. Washington, D.C., 1957.

Hofstadter, Richard. *America at 1750; A Social Portrait*. New York, 1971.

Jordan, John Woolf. *A Description of the State-House, Philadelphia, in 1774*. Reprinted from *The Pennsylvania Magazine of History and Biography*, January 1900.

Josselyn, John. *An Account of Two Voyages to New-England, Made During the Years 1638, 1663*. Boston, 1865. Reprint of London 1675 edition.

Kimball, Fiske. *Domestic Architecture of the American Colonies and of the Early Republic*. New York, 1966. First Edition 1922.

Kouwenhoven, John A. *The Columbia Historical Portrait of New York*. New York, 1953.

Ludwig, Allan I. *Graven Images; New England Stonecarving and Its Symbols, 1650–1815*. Middletown, Conn., 1966.

Mauduit, Israel. *A Short View of the History of the New England Colonies*. 4th ed. London, 1776.

Miller, Perry. *Errand into the Wilderness*. Cambridge, Mass., 1956.

Morrison, Hugh. *Early American Architecture, from the First Colonial Settlements to the National Period*. New York, 1952.

Newhall, Nancy, ed., and Paul Strand, photographer. *Time in New England*. New York, 1950.

Oldmixon, John. *The British Empire in America; Containing the History of the Discovery, Settlement, Progress and Present State of all the British Colonies, on the Continent and Islands of America*. 2 vols. London, 1708.

Pierson, William H., Jr. *American Buildings and Their Architects; The Colonial and Neoclassical Styles*. Garden City, 1970.

Reps, John W. *The Making of Urban America; A History of City Planning in the United States*. Princeton, 1965.

Scully, Vincent. *American Architecture and Urbanism*. New York, 1969.

Shurtleff, Harold R. *The Log Cabin Myth; A Study of the Early Dwellings of the English Colonists in North America.* Gloucester, 1967.

Smith, John. *A Description of New England; or, Observations and Discoveries in the North of America in the Year of Our Lord 1614.* Boston, 1865. Reprint of first edition, London 1616.

Vail, R. G. "The Beginnings of Manhattan," *Journal of the Society of Architectural Historians,* XI, no. 2, 1952, pp. 19–22.

Vaughan, Alden T. *New England Frontier; Puritans and Indians, 1620–1675.* Boston, 1675.

Wood, William. *New England's Prospect; A True, Lively, and Experimental Description of that Part of America, commonly called New England.* Boston, 1898. Reprint of London 1634 edition.